A Fresh Start

111 Affirmations to Make This the Best Year Ever and Create the Life You Want

Karen Carrington

Discovering Diversity Publishing

A Fresh Start – 111 Affirmations to Make This the Best Year Ever and Create the Life You Want

Karen Carrington

Printed in Canada

Third Printing, 2018

ISBN: 9781718187733

This book is dedicated to my two sons who both give me a reason to keep going. Every love story is special, but the love story I have with my two boys is definitely my favorite.

Love, Mom.

Table of Contents

Foreword - Richard Brown

Courage is something that everybody wants — an attribute of good character that makes us worthy of respect. From the Bible to fairy tales, ancient myths to Hollywood movies, our culture is rich with exemplary tales of bravery and self-sacrifice for the greater good. From the cowardly lion in The Wizard of Oz who finds the courage to face the witch, to David battling Goliath in the Bible, to Star Wars and Harry Potter, we have been raised on a diet of heroic and inspirational tales.

Yet courage is not just physical bravery. History books tell colorful tales of social activists, such as Martin Luther King Jr. and Nelson Mandela, who chose to speak out against injustice at great personal risk. Entrepreneurs such as Steve Jobs and Walt Disney, who took financial risks to follow their dreams are like modern-day knights, exemplifying the rewards and public accolades that courage can bring.

Everyone experiences a loss of courage and failure in life. Life is never an unbroken series of victories. We all have setbacks and losses, and sometimes a defeat can seem to overwhelm you. On occasion we bring defeat on ourselves, but more often it is thrust upon us.

In the bible, Job felt overwhelmed. He states, "My days have passed, my plans are shattered, and so are the desires of my heart." (Job 17:1) Have you ever felt like that?

We've all been disappointed at some time in our lives. We've been misled, purposely or unconsciously. We have all stood staring in disbelief at the remains of discarded promises that were made but never kept. The struggle to begin again is a real one when you don't know where to drop your anchor. The heart has a million questions, each one defying your desire to continue on. Love again? Forget it! Why try again? Why believe again when it's been proven you have no guarantees? Why risk your heart's safety once more? Yet it is in daring to leap out in faith that the things we desire are gained.

Where to put our trust becomes the great question. How do we know that we will heal? Live? Love, again and finally be loved in return, the way we've always wanted to be loved? Should promises be taken to heart? How can they be when the record of failure has been so devastating?

If the above correctly describes your thought pattern, this is the perfect read for you. In "A Fresh Start – 111 Affirmations to Make This the Best Year Ever and Create the Life You Want," Karen Carrington places her life experiences on display and goes in depth and presents a very balanced and correct perspective on the issue of failure, faith and the freedom to move forward. I am grateful that God focuses on our faith and not our failures, and as you read you will be reminded that you are more than able to attain your goals despite failure. Failure is one of, if not the best teaching tools that we have.

Carrington reveals personal experiences and tells her personal story of the courage it took to place her life back on the right track to her destiny. Her writing brings great perspective and inspiration for rebuilding our lives after shattered dreams and shortcomings. Chapter 1 sets the precedence for the entire book, The Second Chance. Karen reveals Life Lesson number 1, "God gives us a second chance for a purpose."

Someone has observed that life is like a dollar bill. When you spend money, there are really only one of two ways you can spend it. You can waste it, or you can invest it. The same thing is true with life. Now whether you are young or old, six or sixty, healthy and wealthy, or poor and puny, you can make the rest of your life the best of your life!!

If you, beginning today, would consciously, continuously, constantly, and consistently put first things first, it would absolutely transform your life.

If you are fortunate to live to be 70 years old, you will live approximately 25,567 days. If you are 40 right now you only have 11,000 days left. My suggestion to you regardless of your age is that you make the rest of your life the best of your life. You are steps away from your best life. People often abort their dreams because they lack the patience to go through the necessary process in order to materialize what they see in their heart. "A Fresh Start – 111 Affirmations to Make This the Best Year Ever and Create the Life You Want," challenges us to stay the course of a better life, nothing happens without a process. God is the great orchestrator and after the process you will be developed into the highest form of who you were designed to be—anything else is counterfeit!

I encourage you to start the process NOW, it's your move. In chapter 3, "Making a Move", Carrington reveals Life Lesson #3 "Never allow waiting to become a habit, take risks because life is happening now..."

Karen Carrington is a multi-talented, innovative and inspiring gift to her generation and ultimately the world. God has gifted her to share this powerful tool for overcoming shattered dreams while progressively and courageously committing to consistent self-improvement. Be blessed as you read.

As you prepare to delve into this amazing testimonial of the courage and determination of one woman to make the rest of her life the best of her life, I leave you with the challenge of Chapter 9, Remove, Release and Reset;

"Elevate yourself and do you! Learn to rejoice in the end of toxic relationships and friendships. Letting someone go doesn't mean you don't care about them anymore, in fact, walking away is actually a step forward. Take the time to examine your relationships, friendships, and business partnerships carefully. I guarantee you that when you finally find the courage to let go of what doesn't serve you, it will be one of the most rewarding, most freeing practices in your life. Make this your best year ever."

My prayer is that this book will be a catalyst for you to realize that you can live your best life now. There are great opportunities coming for you up the road...don't quit now. If you Remove, Release and Reset, I guarantee that you will dance about what you once cried about!

-Pastor Richard J. Brown, Founder and Senior Pastor of Kingsway Community Life Centre.

Introduction

I truly want you to jump right into this book but, before you start, I really don't mean to interrupt, but I have a question for you. Have you ever felt extremely excited and motivated? Take a moment and think back to your past when you were really pumped with anticipation and new innovations and creative ideas were blasting out of your brain. Your visions of success were wild and bold and you were determined to achieve them at any cost.

Picture it. You're at the starting line of an important race, the first whistle blows, and you slowly get down on all fours and back your feet onto the starter blocks. Your fingertips are touching the ground; your butt is in the air, and the announcer yells in the megaphone, "On your marks, get set, GO!"

The pistol makes a loud boom, and you dash out of the starting blocks with full force! You're running with grace and maintaining the lead! The crowd is shouting your name as they cheer you on. You're smiling from ear to ear- you've got this! Fifty meters into the race you stumble and collapse to the ground, head over heels. Boom!

With disappointment, you open your eyes staring at the stars, feeling like a complete failure.

This is the same feeling we have when we set out our goals and aim really high! We're super excited to make our dreams come true and when it doesn't work out the way we thought it would, that feeling of defeat and disappointment sinks in. I'm sure your intention was to make it a good year. No wait, better yet, your intention was to make it a fantastic year, but somewhere along the way you lost your bearings and sense of direction. Negativity and fear spin around in your mind. Then you start feeling depleted, discouraged and completely bummed out. Trust me, I've been there. I've ran that race a few times and ended up flat on the ground, bruised, and beaten up.

The fundamental key to reaching your goals, making this the best year ever and creating the life you want is for you to first be very clear of where you are heading. Once you have that all figured out, you can now determine where it is that you need to start. Sometimes, we run races but don't have a distinct starting point and our destination hasn't been clearly defined. The more laser focused you are, the more successful you will be and it's more likely that you will reach your goals. To create the amazing life you want, you first need to discover your true life-purpose. It's important to take action in your life, be intentional about what you want to achieve and stay committed along your life journey. The other key is to love yourself and express love to others while maintaining a positive attitude.

Did you know each and every one of us placed on this planet has a life purpose that is meant to inspire and impact the lives of others in some way? We each have a unique divine gift to share with the world. In the Bible, Romans 12:6 says, "We have different gifts, according to the grace given to each of us." Meaning, we all have a life purpose, some of us know what that is and some of us are still searching to find our calling.

How do you find your life purpose? Ask yourself this question: If money was not an issue, how would I spend my time?

Close your eyes, take a deep breath, and sit with that thought and the sensations. Feel what fires up inside of your soul and then listen to the beat of your heart. What images flash into your mind? Is it traveling overseas? Performing on stage? Building a community centre? Starting your own business or helping the less fortunate? Discovering your truth requires you being 100% authentic with yourself and your desires. When you are living a life of true purpose, you do the things that bring you joy and you begin to surround yourself with the people who support you. Eventually, you begin to pursue your passions.

God and the Universe speak to us all the time through life experiences, giving us clear signs and direction of our life purpose; however, we don't always understand the messages. There are moments in our lives when we know we need to drastically shift the course of our journey in order to be truly happy and create the life we want. When things go 'wrong' in our lives, rather than seeing them as negative experiences, try viewing these obstacles as learning opportunities.

In this book, I reference these obstacles as 'life lessons.' These life lessons help us to wake up and bring awareness to life events. We learn from experiences and make changes for the better. If we look closely,

there is a blessing in every negative situation. When we endure situations that leave us feeling lost or heartbroken such as losing a job, getting evicted, a bad break-up, divorce, miscarriage, financial ruin or addictions, it can leave us feeling ashamed or like we have failed. But guess what? When we run the race of life and fall to the bottom, the good news is that every pitfall has a purpose.

Some life events inflict deep pain, trust me, like I said earlier, I've been there quite a few times, which I will share with you later on in this book. However, I realized my failures were, in fact, learning experiences. God truly turned my messes into a message and my wounds into wisdom.

To progress, we must realize that struggles often lead to a change that allows us to grow, evolve, and finally become who we were meant to be. I had to fall into very dark pits and places to realize that I needed to take a leap of faith, step into my purpose and find my calling. The best things that happened in my life were the painful moments. Although I didn't realize it at the time, these painful life events created a new life path and prepared me for better things. I just had to remove the fear in order to see clearly. We need to break the barriers of fear and take responsibility for creating our destiny because at the end of the day, we are 100% responsible for our own life outcome. You may be born looking like your parents, but you will die looking like your decisions. It's up to you to commit to transform your mindset, to create the life you want and to make it your best year ever!

My childhood, like many others, was filled with many ups and downs; however, over the course of these challenging times, I finally realized I had the power to change my life, my words and my thoughts at any time I chose. I learned to catch my thoughts and stay positive. A shift in my mindset brought a sea of new opportunities through daily affirmations, being positive and remaining goal-oriented. After each failure, I grew much stronger and more resilient. Each time I told myself, "this too shall pass, tough times don't last, tough people do." I would look into the mirror and repeat daily affirmations. My life story was a winding road of trauma, pain, and heartache, but each experience was necessary and helped shape me to be who I am today. I want to share my life experiences in the hopes that my life, some of my darkest and most painful times, and the ways that I found my way out of them will bring healing and will be the key that can unlock someone else's prison.

When I turned 40, I had a beautiful birthday bash. It was such a special day that I will never ever forget. Friends, family, catered food, gorgeous décor, amazing music, my hot pink glam dress, live guest performances, door prizes; I went all out and pulled out all the stops! It was lit! That night was a pivotal point in my life because the number 40 is a very powerful number. Did you know that the number 40 is the only number that is spelled with each letter appearing in alphabetical order? No other number does that! Not 14, not 23, not 75. No other number but 40. Think about it for a second...F...O... R... T...Y. Pretty cool huh?!? And you know what? For me, that symbolized that my life was ready to be in 'divine order'. It was that night that I made a conscious, intentional decision to create the life I want. Instead of worrying and focusing on negative thoughts, I decided to enjoy the roller-coaster ride of life while embracing all the ups and downs it offered. Even if I got a little tripped up and shaken after a traumatic life event, it was a wild ride! I learned that everything happens for a reason and it always happens for my ultimate good. These life events weren't happening to me, rather they were happening for me. When that 'negative committee' in my head acted up and tried to hold a 'negativity meeting', I shut it right down! These voices really need to take a back seat because I know my life situations always turn out with a positive outcome. When I fail or make a mistake, I look for the lesson and learn from it. Yes, it may set me back a few steps, but I make the effort to pick myself up and get back into the game. I don't wither up and play victim. Nope. Not a chance. Yes, I feel sad and I grieve, but I don't stay stuck in that place. I dust myself off, slip on a pair of powerhouse stilettos, straighten that invisible bling crown on my golden blonde hair and spritz on some sweet-smelling confidence! I take a good hard look in the mirror and affirm, "I am bold, beautiful and strong. I am golden. I shine like the sun. I am a bad azz rock star. I persevere. I am relentless. I am fierce. I can do absolutely anything I set my mind to."

The personal stories in this book illustrate my journey, the trials and tribulations, the goals I set and the lessons I have learned. This book has 11 chapters; 11 vivid snap shots of some of my different life stories. I fell on my face eleven times and got back up twelve (well to be honest, I fell on my face way more than 11 times, but I chose these particular stories for this book; the others I've saved for the next one! Wink, wink, nudge, nudge!) I also shared 111 affirmations and 11 life lessons in this book that helped sculpt me... and if you're reading this book, I believe you desire to make a life shift too. Are you ready to have your best year ever and create the life that YOU want? I bet you are! I'm looking forward to embarking on this journey with you! Let's do this!

Each morning is a fresh start and every day brings new opportunities. It's important to start our day with authentic intentions and positive affirmations. Let me break it down for you. Firstly, 'an intention' helps create more clarity in your life.

Setting an intention is like drawing a map of where you wish to go- it becomes the driving force of your higher consciousness.

Without an intention, there is no map or destination, and you're just driving down a road aimlessly.

An affirmation is a declaration that something is true. It's a positive, empowering statement that helps us achieve success in our lives. Affirmations are short yet powerful sentences and they have the ability to program our minds into believing the statement.

If a negative belief is deeply rooted in our subconscious mind, then it has the ability to over-ride positive affirmations. Affirmations are challenging for some people because their negative thought patterns are so strong that they defeat the effect of the positive statement. For affirmations to be effective, they need to be repeated and written down frequently. They are to be said in the present tense with the intention to follow through with the statement.

The goal is to clear your mind completely and declare affirmations in a quiet space. Hey, you can even play meditation music if you wish! As the days and weeks go by, your mind will shift.

The 111 affirmations and 11 life lessons throughout this book are shared to help you navigate through life's challenges and reach your goals. With practice, you will witness the unfolding of your best year ever and create the life you want. I also encourage you to refer to the affirmations referenced after each chapter and meditate on a few of them each day. This helped me navigate through life's stresses, begin each day with a "Fresh Start" and reach my goals. I have included lined pages throughout this book at the end of each chapter and a complimentary journal at the end of this book as a gift from me to you! I encourage you to use these pages to make personal notes, track your goals and write out your favorite affirmations. This way, you can easily refer back to them. These notes will help you document where you are now, and you will quickly see at a glance where you want to go in your future.

Below is the first affirmation. Yes, it's a bit longer than the other 110 of them throughout the book. I know it seems like a lot, but I personally say it out loud daily and it has brought prosperity and abundance to my life. Therefore, I want you to start EACH day, yes, each day and declare this affirmation with conviction. As the days go by, it will become second nature:

A Fresh Start- Affirmation #1

"Today, I am open and ready for the prosperity and blessings that are coming my way. I am an amazing person who is loveable and deserves to be loved. I let go of all past hurts and pain. I am focused on shifting my mindset into a positive space. I possess the qualities needed to be extremely successful, and I am committed to making this year my best year ever. I choose to stop apologizing for being me, and today, I will say this with ease, being guilt free, that if it doesn't feel right, I will not do it. Starting today, I am dedicated to making this positive shift in my life as I focus all my energy on a fantastic year ahead. As my beautiful life unfolds, I welcome new ideas. Today, my mind is open as I clearly visualize the happiness and abundance I desire. I manifest an energy of love. I attract healthy frequencies and positive vibrations into my life. I will unlock new possibilities by being open to new beginnings.

Today is a new day with new opportunities for a fresh start."

Chapter 1-
The Second Chance

Nearly every night I had vivid nightmares of my father trying to hurt me in some way. I would wake up sweaty and my pajamas were soaking wet. I peed the bed constantly and quickly stuffed the wet sheets in the laundry hamper hoping my parents wouldn't find out I peed the bed yet again. These constant nightmares were the result of the ongoing days of emotional neglect I had endured from my father. I would dread waking up after these horrible dreams because I would have to face the reality of a new day.

As I slipped out of bed each morning, I expected it would be another day of verbal put downs, emotional neglect, or perhaps a black eye just like the one I got once for having a friend over at the house unannounced.

My childhood was unstable and dysfunctional; I was always in fear and constantly sad. I cried incessantly and tried to figure out new ways to feel accepted. I cared so much what my parents thought about me, but I always felt like a failure. I never felt good enough. I never felt I had my parent's approval. I did well in school. I was active, athletic and didn't smoke or do drugs! I tried to figure out new ways to do better, be better and get their attention, but I seemed to always fall short. I felt unworthy and just wanted the pain to go away forever.

One late summer evening I sat at the edge of my bed and looked out my bedroom window as the sun was setting. I felt numb and emotionless inside. I was 15 and was hopeless. Without much thought, I left the house and walked to the community elementary school. I looked around, and I realized there weren't any people nearby, the neighbourhood was unusually quiet that evening. As I walked, everything around me: the trees, the sound of the birds, everything... it all seemed insignificant to me. Thoughts of being verbally abused and feeling unworthy circled in my mind, and I felt disconnected, like I didn't belong, like I didn't matter.

I continued to walk towards the school, managed to climb up the fifty-foot building and stood at the very top. The numb feeling was still there. I was despondent. I slowly looked down and thought to myself about how I hated my life. I wanted the pain and loneliness to end. I tilted my head forward and glanced down again as the feelings of inadequacy consumed me. "There's no point being alive. Why am I even here?" I couldn't stand living anymore. My childhood was a constant emotionally and verbally abusive battle that I could never win. I never heard the words *"I love you"* from my father- not once growing up. I do not know, even now, what those words sound like from a father. I, of course, heard them from outside men and boys who I looked to for love, but never once from my father. I did not receive emotional support from my mother, either. She was passive about the things that went on between my father and I, perhaps she had to protect her marriage? Perhaps she felt awkward? Perhaps I wasn't worth the fight? I will never know.

I didn't know how to deal with these feelings so escaping them was the best way and only way I knew how to handle them. Continuing my life was unbearable. I closed my eyes, and I walked closer edge of the rooftop, slowly placing one foot in front of the other. I looked down and I jumped. I screamed all the way down.

SPLAT....

I landed face down flat on the cold cement. Knocked out. Stars spinning. Blood flowing.

Hours later, I opened my eyes, I was lying in a hospital bed. I was disappointed and thought to myself. "Damn it, I'm still alive." A nurse walked towards me with a clipboard in her hand. She explained that a young man had found me at the school yard, and he called the ambulance for help. Then, she gently whispered in my ear, "Sweetheart, your father is here to see you." For a moment, I was so happy inside, nervous, but nevertheless, I figured I was going to get his attention. "My dad's here to save me!"

My father walked towards me with his hands in his pockets. The nurse excused herself to give us privacy. He looked down at me as I lay in the bed and said, "You jumped? Get up, we're going home." My heart sank. I thought to myself, "I'm such a loser. I can't do anything right; sh*t, I can't even kill myself right." We never spoke of that day, again.

Time had passed and because this issue was never addressed, I ran away from home several times, for months at a time. I lived in shelters and shared showers and common rooms; I sometimes stayed at the YMCA. I would stay at random friends' homes or in stranger's homes to escape from the pain. But, running away was just a temporary solution to a seemingly never-ending problem.

My parents migrated to Canada from Trinidad and tried to integrate into the North American way of living while raising me and my siblings. My mother had wonderful qualities; she was charismatic, vibrant and super funny! She had lots of friends in her business and social network and she loved to travel. She put me in baseball and was my coach for years. She had me in ballet, and she brought me on trips with her. These activities kept me occupied, but for me, as a child, I needed a sense of deeper security from my mother. I yearned for her to protect me from my father's behaviours, and I needed to know (or at least feel) that everything would be ok. But, we never talked about it. We never talked about anything that happened between myself and my father. I was always in an anxiety ridden state, and they never sought out help or therapy for me.

My father was very strict. I wasn't allowed to interact with boys, and phone calls were to be kept to a minimum. I am not sure why some of the things transpired in our home because we never spoke of family issues. They were off limits, and emotional, financial and family topics were shoved under the rug. I think my parents were probably under the stress of finances because the paper route money that I earned was counted by my parents, and then I never saw it again. There was often thick tension in the house, and as a child, I absorbed this tension which led to me always being in an anxious state. I could not have friends over to my house, and I had to be home straight after school each day. I purposely joined every sport and activity at school to avoid going home and running into my father who was often in and out of the house due to his unpredictable working hours.

As a teen, I felt restricted and didn't have an outlet to express myself, to develop or feel heard. Because I never heard the words *"I love you"* from my father, I felt unworthy, unimportant and invisible. It became exhausting to please him and as a result I started to hang around boys and make out with these guys who I felt "loved" me. So now I went from being 'the good girl' to 'the naïve girl' who needed attention. I would sneak out of the house to meet up with them (I used to be a pro at jumping out of windows!). I would sometimes spend the night out, not return back home and would end up being late for class the next morning. My marks started to slip in the 10th grade. As a result, my father thought it was best that I was placed in all girl's private school. When I got the news, I cried for days in my room. I felt like I just received a guilty verdict after a court case and was being shipped off to jail.

The private school was a 1.5-hour bus ride to and from school each day, then I had to walk up a steep hill for 20 more minutes. It was awful in the winter time. I was not allowed to wear make up and was stuck wearing a green plaid uniform with brown loafer shoes. Um hello!? Not fashionable at all. The school looked like a bed and breakfast building with creepy vines on the side of the stone walls. It was gloomy inside, and the floors creaked. The school only had approximately 10 students in each grade. It felt like prison for me because I was a social butterfly! Some of the girls in my class were brought up in a sheltered environment and had never even kissed a boy nor did they want to. When we would chat at lunch time, some of them said they had no interest in boys because they never engaged with boys growing up (they had been in an all girls school all of their lives). I thought to myself, "Aw man, I am not going to make it out of here alive."

As a result of these childhood experiences, I developed very low self-esteem. When I would cry as a young girl, my father would call me "marshmallow"; I was soft, overweight, sensitive and weak. I held on to the fear to make me feel safe instead of trying to find a way to feel confident. As a young girl, I felt as though fear was always there for me, and it never let me down because it was a safe, comforting feeling and I knew I could run to it. Fear was my ally, and it was always there when I needed a dose of it. For me, having confidence was too risky because getting close to someone or wanting love would often lead to rejection. But, fear and distress were easily achievable.

Fear was like a high. Fear was my drug of choice.

Although I was always scared and felt unloved, unworthy, and unimportant, something deep down inside of me knew, even as a child, that I was meant to live that day I tried to end my life. I was not sup- posed to die. I knew I was put on this planet for a purpose. There was always this voice in my head telling me I was meant to do something spectacular. That voice was so faint but loud enough to keep me going.

Do you ever hear that voice? That one that tells you to keep pushing through no matter what? Don't ignore it. That's the voice that keeps you going when everything seems impossible. It's that voice that says, "I am meant to live a life with purpose. I am meant to do something great, I am meant to have a second chance."

Life Lesson #1:

When we are given a second chance at life, it is not to be taken for granted. God gives us a second chance for a purpose. Second chances are a gift from the Universe and serve as opportunities for a fresh start and to live a life of abundance.

Today is a new day, another chance to accomplish your goals. In the space provided below, write down the goals you want to accomplish this year.

_____

_____

_____

_____

_____

_____

_____

_____

_____

_____

_____

_____

_____

_____

Second Chance Affirmations

2. I can clearly see the new beginnings around me.

3. I deserve another chance at life.

4. Powerful changes are happening; I welcome and embrace them.

5. I can conquer the clutter and create order in my life.

6. With passion and joy, I am embracing this second chance.

7. Today is a new day, I will try something new.

8. God is a God of second chances.

9. Today is a fresh start, a new 24 hours.

10. I grab new opportunities with both hands.

11. I walk confidently today. I am thankful for this new day.

Chapter 2-
The Early Miracle

As my teen years went on, my home life didn't change. I was eighteen and ended up getting pregnant. I felt excited because I thought that this pregnancy and new baby would give me the unconditional love I was seeking and the validation that I desperately needed. My parents were disappointed and didn't support me, so I left home and moved in with the father of my child.

I was only twenty-six weeks pregnant when my water broke, and I was rushed to the hospital. I went into labour with an emergency C-section. Within hours, my son was born premature, weighing only 1 pound 7 ounces. The size of a tiny stick of butter. My mind was hysterical; everything was moving so fast. The nurses scurried around me, and I knew at that very moment that something was terribly wrong. He was born with many health complications that were life threatening. He underwent open heart surgery, had a lung infection, used a ventilator to breathe and was fed with tubes. He was deaf in one ear, had jaundice, and developed a hernia due to stress. Laser surgery was performed on his eyes because he had a disease which causes abnormal blood vessels to grow in the retina. This growth can cause the retina to detach from the back of the eye, leading to blindness. He was scheduled for endless blood transfusions and suffered severe weight loss. Every ounce he lost was a step closer to death.

The surgeon sadly told me he wouldn't make it. "No!" I pleaded, "he has to make it! Why did he come out premature?" I had so many questions.

You know what? I never got the answer to this mystery. I questioned God and why this was happening to me. "Please don't let him die. Please God, if you do me this one favour, I swear, I'll never be bad again. C'mon God please, work with me here! Don't let me down." Each day, despite many ups and downs, my baby became stronger and he survived! My miracle baby made it through, he beat the odds! He is a true survivor, and still 'til today, at 23 years old, he is a fighter that overcomes all obstacles that are thrown his way. He is an outstanding, honest, handsome, polite, young man with integrity and an obsession with cars, the rapper Eminem and bubble tea (weird combo, I know, don't ask. I guess it's a preemie thing).

My precious baby boy entered this world on a day that I believe is powerfully symbolic. He was born on January 11th and as you know, that calendar date is written as 1/11. For me, the number 1 represents the start of something new and fresh beginnings. Many claim that the number 111 is a message from the angels and it's the angels' way of telling us that our desires are about to be manifested. It's a mystical message to pay close attention to our thoughts and emotions. For me, the number 111 represented the survival of my angel baby and the number has blessed the title of this book. It's the day my miracle angel baby arrived and was here to stay.

So let's get back to the story. As an infant, my son remained in the hospital for almost a year as I lived with his father without my parent's support. It was a tough time. My parents were still really disappointed in me for getting pregnant at such a young age. My mother stopped contacting me, and my father moved out of the country. Neither parent ever visited my son and I in the hospital. In fact, even as twenty more years passed, my father still never met my son.

Our baby was finally released from the hospital and a few months later, my son's father ended up moving back in with his parents on very short notice. We were teen parents, paying rent and taking care of a preemie baby, and it was very stressful. So when he informed me that it was best he moved back home, I was devastated, lost and alone. How was I going to manage as a single mother? I found a part time job at the local mall, quickly applied for government social assistance with a 'single mother' status and found a new apartment in government housing in a tough area. I was a teenage mother now on my own to raise my preemie son. I felt abandoned, and I resented my situation.

I questioned why this was happening to me. I wanted to have a pity party for myself, but I didn't allow that to happen. As tempting as it was, I had to keep pushing forward. I refrained from staying in a victim mentality by making my physical, mental and spiritual health a priority. I went to the gym and invested in myself. I decided to take a few courses to elevate myself, I wrote down my life goals, I prayed, went to church and declared daily affirmations. Self-pity keeps us stuck and let's be honest, staying stuck is the easy way out. It prevents us from getting up and moving forward.

Sick child and all, I had to keep it moving. I continued to work part time and I went to hair school to better myself and get my hairstylist cosmetology license. Things were going pretty well until one day, out of nowhere, my son's father subpoenaed me with paperwork stating my son wasn't receiving quality care from me and that he needed to be taken away from me urgently. He only gave me one week to find a lawyer. The court date was set for the next week! How was I going to get that done!? He took me to court and he wanted full custody of our son. "What??? Why?? I'm a wonderful mother! Why is this happening to me?" I just want a life of peace. I didn't allow this situation to bring me down. I kept my head high and went through the court motions with faith. Although I was afraid and caught off guard, I had to believe that everything would work out in my favour. I prayed every night and stayed strong. My lawyer insisted I fill out documents and only gave me a few days to do so which would help plead my case. There were so many hoops to jump through. It was a tremendous amount of pressure and extremely overwhelming. I had to get a series of signatures, many forms needed to be filled out for Legal Aid and I had to run around and collect affidavits.

I reached out to friends and they offered me support. They were a listening ear and were there for me. My son's teachers and the school principal and his family doctor all wrote positive reinforcing affidavits on my behalf stating I was a wonderful mother and that I would never mistreat my son and that he lived in a safe, loving home. It was a comforting feeling to receive this outpouring of love. My lawyer reassured me every step of the way that everything would be fine if I just remained calm and stated the truth. He said, "Karen, the truth always comes to light." I continued to pray that week and I repeated Psalm 27:1 which says "the Lord is my light and my salvation, whom shall I fear?" I remained patient and faithful. Then, one day, out of the blue, my son's father made a decision to award me sole custody of my son and just like that, the battle against me was over. He dropped the case. The court proceedings had stopped. And this chapter was now closed.

Hebrews 11:1 says, "To have faith is to be sure of the things we hope for, to be certain of the things we cannot see." Unfortunately, some people don't believe in things that they cannot see. There's an enormous level of importance attributable to having faith in life. When we hold unwavering faith, we attract good things because we believe and expect in good things to come. Gratitude and faith shifts your focus from what your life lacks to the abundance that is already present. When we are afraid of the unknown, having faith and practicing the art of gratitude takes us to a place of peace. Live your life as if everything is a miracle. My son was my early miracle. Finally years later, my son's father and I made amends. There was forgiveness, healing and closure. A Fresh Start

Life Lesson #2:

Facing adversity happens to all of us. Getting stuck is not the prob- lem. Staying stuck is. Today and every day, practice the art of gratitude and have faith in the things that are unknown.

What are you grateful for today, right now, at this very moment?

Write down the things that you are grateful for.

_____

_____

_____

_____

_____

_____

_____

_____

_____

_____

_____

_____

_____

_____

Affirmations for Faith

12. The outer world cannot shake my inner peace.

13. As I breathe in I am calm, as I breathe out I smile.

14. I trust that all is well, and everything is working out for my highest and greatest good.

15. Whatever I am going through is guiding me to where I want to go.

16. I go with the flow; my life is easy and filled with joy.

17. Whatever I ask for in prayer, I believe I have received it, I believe it will be mine.

18. I am protected; I am safe. This too shall pass.

19. Gratitude and faith flow through my mind and body like a clear, healing stream.

20. I do not waiver or doubt, I ask in faith and I there- fore receive.

21. I let go and trust it's all happening perfectly.

Chapter 3-
Making a Move

I was a young, single mother, and my son was now six. I was on social assistance and would juggle many odd jobs all at once to make ends meet. I worked in beauty salons, the mall and in a night club serving drinks as a shooter girl. Oh gawsh, listen, I had like zero experience being a server. So here I am in a smoky night club balancing wobbly trays with the fragile glasses filled to the rim with liquor. I would spend the entire night trying to navigate through the packed crowd with loud bass booming and blinding strobe lights flashing everywhere! It was totally brutal for me, but I managed. I just smiled, served the drinks and stuffed the cash in my leather thigh high boots 'til I collected over $300 in profits! At the end of my shift at 2 a.m., I jumped in a cab and went home quite pleased with my accomplishments! I balanced all these jobs as I raised my son. Boy, I really knew how to survive; I was a true hustler. I learned these skills as a child living under my father's strict regime. I developed a natural survival skill with the mindset of "I've got to make it through today by any means necessary. I gotta stay above water."

But trust me, it wasn't easy. I'm telling you, at times, I was oh so close to going down some very sketchy paths. My street friends from the night club scene offered me some opportunities to make fast illegal cash, but it wasn't for me. Yeah, hey, I made some regrettable choices at that age that I'm not so proud of, but I knew that the illegal shady stuff just wasn't what I was all about so I declined. As difficult as my life was, I yearned for something more, something meaningful and more challenging. Day after day, I would think to myself, "I know there's something bigger out there for me but jeez man, where on earth do I start looking? The library? The classified section in the newspapers? The yellow pages?"

I mulled over different avenues to find a new job and to discover a new life that would push and stretch me. I wanted a fresh start. One day, I sat on the couch and watched my son lay on the purple area rug by my feet quietly playing with his toy cars. I watched him weave the cars through the patterns on the rug; he was so peaceful. As I observed him slowly falling asleep, I thought it would be a great time to call my neighbour as he napped. I dialed her number and she picked up immediately! Oh, how I loved her. She always gave me great advice, so when she answered, I was thrilled! I told her that I wanted to research a project but needed some information and background. (She was eating and chewing in my ear while we spoke but that didn't bother me, we were so comfortable with each other.) She swallowed her food, took a sip of her drink and said, "Girl, check this out. I heard about this new cool web-based invention thing, um what's that thingy called again, um, the internet? Yes, that's it. It's this world wide web thingy. You have to get yourself a computer! Come over and try mine in the meantime 'til you get one. Trust me; it will change your life! I'll make you some food too!"

The next day, I headed over to her place and I was ready for my tutorial. Wow! This was overwhelming. I didn't know much about the internet back in the early nineties, but I quickly jumped on that internet band wagon! I was at her house every day after work and watched as she web-surfed around the world. I was convinced. I was hooked. I was sold! I went out to buy an inexpensive computer from a local pawn shop and set it up at home. Man, was it a struggle! I didn't know how to use the mouse; the left click function was awkward, the wires from the keyboard and monitor were all so confusing, but I was determined! Finally, the screen turned on, and I was exposed to a whole new world. "Yes!" I screamed. "Yesssss!! I love this!"

I stayed up all night clicking away. I enjoyed the new world that was now available at my fingertips. OMG! There were online coupons, mega sales, travel ideas, new online friends, but all the annoying pop up porn sites totally irritated me. I wasn't into that stuff and these annoying sites and pop ups slowed down my searches and froze up the screen. I quickly learned and made a mental note to self to stop clicking on suspicious fishy looking links!

I covered my eyes and screeched as racy photos and videos appeared across my screen "Oh gawsh, please! How do I make these pop ups go away?! HEEEELLPP!" I quickly called a friend and explained my embarrassing situation. He laughed and explained to me the important ins and outs of how to safely navigate through the internet. He warned me of online scams, predators, stalkers and fake profiles. Today, as I look back, I laugh! I was such a naïve novice! Lesson learned.

Anyways, I continued my quest for a new, exciting life and quickly made new friends online. I lived in Ottawa but always fantasized about the city of Toronto. My dream was to live in the urban metropolitan city of multiculturalism and diversity. I wanted to live right near the CN tower. There was nowhere else I wanted to be.

Growing up in Ottawa was much too quiet and conservative for me. I was an energetic, vibrant, fashionista, glamour girl who was ready to survive a new hustle and fast paced life that I was meant to have. I remember many people telling me not to move. My mother thought I was crazy for moving to the "crazy city," and she was not supportive. Some friends thought it was too risky because I didn't have a job and was starting from scratch. Many people warned me not to move but a girlfriend of mine told me, "Karen, if your dreams are big, people will mock you for them. Forget those people; they will not help you succeed. Go and do you."

The father of my son and his parents were constantly bringing ongoing, unbearable, toxic conflict to my life. I wasn't receiving any child support from him and I was feeling defeated from the constant arguments (I was in hair school full time and working so many jobs, the conflict was breaking me down). I knew it was not a healthy situation. I knew I needed a change of environment. So,

I prayed and asked God for guidance to help me set out a plan to make a move and start over. I went through the motions, following God's lead, step by step and did not allow doubt or fear to creep in. I gave 60 days' notice to my landlord (who tried to convince me to stay; she really loved me as a tenant and warned me that it would be challenging to make it in the big city. I thanked her but continued on with my pursuit). I contacted friends to help me pack, I renewed my driver's license that had expired, I checked and double checked that I had all my hours completed in hair school, I wrote my exam and graduated with Honours. I had a beautiful party in my backyard with my friends, I will never forget that party, and that pretty baby blue floral dress that I wore. Everyone was laughing, and I had such a good time. I remember they pinned me down to the grass and tried to get me to smoke pot as a token of one last good bye, but I closed my lips shut frantically swinging my head back and forth. I refused but was laughing so hard...I will never forget that party. Seeing my closest friends from the neighbourhood there for me... that truly meant a lot.

Everything fell smoothly into place; all loose ends were now tied and I was ready to move to Toronto with my son. I felt confident with my decision. I knew it was the right thing to do. My son was young but extremely excited for the new adventure we were about to embark on. I jumped into a moving van with a very good friend of mine who offered to help drive, and we were off into the sunset. A new chapter of my life was beginning, and I was excited to see what was unfolding.

We arrived safely in Toronto, and everything seemed like it was coming together for me until the roommate, who I met online and who was supposed to split the cost of rent bailed in our first week of living in the apartment. This, of course, caught me off guard. (I never heard from that person, again. They had personal issues they had to deal with.) "Jeez man, seriously. This is crazy! I'm out half the flipping rent!" I was off to a bad start.

I walked up and down the streets in our neighbourhood called "Jane and Finch" where I lived (known as a very rough part of Toronto). I was looking for work to supplement the additional costs I gained when my roommate bailed. I did odd jobs, here and there, to get by. I knew I had to make it work and, indeed, I did! I landed a job in an upscale, glamourous salon downtown Toronto. And, not too shortly after my successful job search, I ended up meeting a nice man, and we got married the first year I moved to Toronto. It all happened so fast and looking back now, I believe inside I wanted to fill a void in my life. We had another son, and then I landed a permanent government job, and we moved into a house. "Praise God! I finally have a family, a home, love, and my children are happy!" It was a dream come true on the outside. Unfortunately, on the inside, the harsh reality was that I never dealt with my inner issues that I ran away from. I thought I was happy, but I still had internal battles of insecurity, low self-esteem and fears that I was suppressing from my childhood. I couldn't cope with every day simple life issues and started to break down weekly. This was a rocky time but at least I had everything I wanted, or at least what I thought I wanted. Only time would tell. The truth of the matter is that regardless of these ill feelings surfacing, I was still really, super proud that I made the brave move to Toronto to follow my dreams. Fear can be a limiting factor but moving past that fear is essential for success. Ignore everybody who tries to tell you what to do or think. Follow your own instincts and goals because staying complacent never led anybody to greatness.

Life Lesson #3:

Never allow waiting to become a habit. Take risks because life is happening now. Let go of the need to feel comfortable.

Is there an area in your life where you need to step out of your comfort zone and try something new? Make a list below of dreams you want to accomplish.

_____

_____

_____

_____

_____

Affirmations for Moving Forward

22. All my choices are in agreement with my desires.

23. As I choose my thoughts, I choose my life.

24. Each day I choose to see things from the most optimistic perspective.

25. Each decision I make presents wondrous new possibilities.

26. Every day I have the option to make choices that support my well-being.

27. Every moment of my life is full of choices

28. I always choose the bolder option.

29. I always have the choice to recreate my reality.

30. I always have the freedom to choose.

31. I choose to accept only those beliefs which empower my life.

Chapter 4-
The Celebration of Life

I lived with anxiety for years, and I was extremely unhappy and depressed in my marriage. To add to this pain, in the summer of 2011, my mother passed away from diabetes at the young age of 58. She was found collapsed on the floor, alone in her apartment, in Ottawa by a nurse who was checking in on her during a routine in-house visit. Losing my mother so suddenly felt like my whole world had been totally turned upside down. I had never experienced a loss like that before. I remember receiving the call from my cousin when I was at work. As she spoke, I felt completely numb, like I didn't deserve happiness, as though I was being robbed of joy. I slowly put down the phone and I told a colleague about the news I just received. She sat me down in her private office, poured me water and started to console me. I had so many mixed emotions-the feelings of shock and confusion were spinning inside me. I questioned God. "Why did she have to go at such a young age? What was she feeling when she took her last breath? Was she sad? Was she scared?" I couldn't stop crying, my head was buried in my lap, and I wouldn't look up. I left the office early that day and took the train to meet my cousin who offered me support. I remember that train ride so vividly. I wiped the tears from my face with the palm of my trembling hands. I saw the scenery out the window: the trees, nature all around, but as I gazed out the window, my heart was so heavy, and though I knew that dealing with grief was a reality we all face at some point, I just wasn't ready to hear my mother was gone forever.

The experience of grief is different for everyone. For me, I lost a lot of weight and was in a constant daze. I remember driving, once, and stopping my car at a GREEN light! I put my foot on the brakes in the middle of the intersection! It was crazy! I quickly snapped out of this zombie state and proceeded through the lights with tears running down my cheeks and thought to myself, "Ok Karen, this is pathetically embarrassing. You're losing it girl; get it together." The grief I faced was heavy, and to make matters worse, my marriage was shaky.

On the day of my mother's funeral, which was held in Ottawa, many of her loved ones were there. The room was packed. My best friend drove from Toronto to Ottawa to surprise me! I saw her pull up in the funeral parking lot minutes before the service began, my heart filled with comfort. We ran towards each other and she hugged me so hard. It meant the world to me.

It was so nice to see old friends and family back home from Ottawa and the support was overwhelming, but there were some aspects of the funeral that were not a good experience. There was conflict with my grandmother; she was hurt by some of the details of the funeral arrangements. She felt left out of the planning process and took it out on me and my siblings. Harsh, hurtful things were said to us, and she cancelled the reception that was to be held at her house. I thought to myself, "How could my grandmother do this, it's her own daughter's funeral?" There was thick heavy tension in the room. My siblings and cousins quickly had to collaborate, make alternate reception arrangements, buy food and drinks all while maintaining our composure in front of the guests. In addition to that chaos, there was a typo on the front of the funeral program which was my fault. "How did I miss that detail? I'm such a perfectionist. Damn it! How did that slip by me?" I felt such shame. I was supposed to pay attention to every detail and that was out of my character. I felt as though I dishonoured her. I tried to shake it off, but I felt like I screwed up.

I was really hard on myself throughout the grief process. I was really stuck in a bad place. But eventually as time went by, I began to let that feeling of shame go. A pastor at my church gave me great advice and said that we can't undo the past, the past is done; those things happened, and I needed to forgive my grandmother, and moreover, I needed to forgive myself. I became more compassionate with myself, forgave and moved on. I reflect back to the funeral day with a new, positive mindset. I focus on the positive aspects. The fact that I stood up in front of everyone and delivered a beautiful eulogy for my mom-I truly honoured her that day. My sister brought an elegant cake and she sang a song with her angelic voice as a tribute. My brother shared beautiful memories of our mom and his wife organized many of the funeral details and kept everything in check. Also, my family was able to come together at my cousin's house, we had awesome moments at the reception and ate great food. We laughed, made jokes and shared fond memories of my mother just like she would have wanted. She was always the life of the party! This day was a true Celebration of Life!

After my mother's passing, I signed up for a grief support group at my church which was really helpful. I left the sessions feeling much better and much lighter. I would go home, look at old pictures of my mother, play songs that reminded me of her and gaze at my eyes in the mirror. I had her eyes. She always told me that she loved my eye lashes so much. She said they were so pretty. I cherish that compliment from her. I believe she wanted to tell me more nice things, but deep inside, she was hurting.

My mother was an amazing woman, but she didn't often show much affection to me. I understand why, now. Deep wounds often hinder us from being capable of showing love. I believe my mother was hurting inside, perhaps from her marriage, her job, her family, finances or it could be a combination of other things. I will never truly know why. But when people are deeply hurt inside, it is often difficult for them to show affection. Being raised in a West Indian home by parents from Trinidad, we as children often weren't told what was truly happening behind the scenes. It was taboo for parents to share details or information about the problems, secrets, or family issues with the children. (I really wanted to break that cycle. As I raised my kids, I allowed a very open dialogue between myself and my 2 sons).

Nine months after her death, on Mother's Day, I got a large tattoo on my leg in memory of my mother. It was a beautiful bouquet of flowers with the word "Mom" scripted in elegant, bold letters across it. I lay there as the tattoo artist worked away at her art. She heard me cry, quietly. I wasn't crying because of the pain of the tattoo, but from the pain that my mother was really gone. Although my mother wasn't largely emotionally present in my life, she provided me the essentials- I had a roof over my head, she fed me, and she always tried her best to make my birthday parties and holidays special. She was really funny, charismatic and had soooo many friends who absolutely loved being around her. The tattoo artist held my hand as I stared at the ceiling. Tears flowed down my cheeks. I reflected on the loss of my mother and how I had to forgive her for the times she didn't protect me from my father. That moment, and others like it, taught me a lot about my past emotional issues regarding my mother.

Today, I see my mom as my angel looking down at me from above in everything that I do. She has given me so many gifts that I use today like her charisma, her witty nature and her social butterfly-ness. I carry her communication skills and speaking talents. She excelled in her Business Communication course in college and spoke internationally with her Toastmasters group.

Toastmasters is a nonprofit educational organization that operates clubs around the world for the purpose of helping members improve their communication and public speaking skills. She was at the top of the ladder in her District. She was a DTM which stands for Distinguished Toast Master. This title represents the highest level of educational achievement in the Toastmasters organization. To earn the DTM designation, one must earn the Competent Communicator and Leader award, serve at least six months as a club officer, complete one-year term as a district officer, be a mentor and coach and participate in Success Planning. When I did this research, it hit me. Whoa! I saw myself in my mother. I made the connection to my gift. Currently, in my life, I have my own talk show, and I am an Inspirational Speaker. When I am on stage speaking or live on air on my show, I know I make her proud. Realizing how my mother lived and who my mother really was gave me the opportunity to gain some closure. I realized that she and her gifts live on through me. I also realized that she was a woman with real feelings just like me. I don't have an explanation why she didn't assist me with my dad, but I no longer need one. I am proud to be her daughter and it's an honour to continue her legacy of personal improvement and touching the lives of others.

When we lose someone we love, it is important to continue living and not lose ourselves in suffering. Grief teaches us that joy and pain can in fact coexist. By working through the death of a loved one, one day you will come to a place of acceptance, and you will eventually see how far you've come. You will be stronger and know a strength that you never knew was there to begin with. Hold on to that strength because you never know when you might need it again. I certainly did.

Life Lesson #4:

When your loved one has passed, although there is pain, continue to live your life to the fullest as this is the greatest way to honour and celebrate their life.

Is there pain, loss or hurt that you are currently holding onto? Is it making you continue to suffer unnecessarily? Write down some of these memories. Reflect on them and begin to release them.

_____

_____

_____

_____

_____

_____

_____

Affirmations for Grief and Loss

32. In my sadness, I am patient with my healing process.

33. I let go of my sorrow, but I hold onto my love for my loved one.

34. I'm surrounded by support, seen and unseen.

35. I choose to heal my hurt spirit. I will feel my grief but not wallow in it

36. Grieving takes time.

37. I feel my angels holding me, today, as I grieve.

38. I accept what I cannot change and find the courage to change the things I can.

39. I rest when I need it. I am gentle with myself as I heal.

40. I am thankful for the time I shared with my loved one.

41. I can pay tribute by living my own life in a beautiful way.

Chapter 5-
Fifty Shades of Clear

The anxiety that I dealt with from childhood continued during my marriage. Anxious thoughts of not feeling loveable, special or wanted filled my head daily, and they were depleting me. Negative thoughts of feeling like I wasn't important to anyone and what I had to say didn't matter caused me serious internal pain and anguish. I thought my ideas weren't logical or relevant and my comments didn't make grammatical sense. Every time I had a conversation with someone that required some depth, the voices in my head would say, "Karen, do you seriously think this person in front of your face is even listening to you? Do you think they even understand what you are blabbing on about like a stammering fool, I mean seriously, look at the expression on their face, Karen. They think you're dumb and uneducated. Karen, honestly, you just don't make sense." I would agree with the voice in my head and say, "yep, you're right, they think I'm an idiot, so how do I get out of this? How can I escape this conversation and redeem myself as a worthy person? How do I convince people that I can have a relevant dialogue and make them see that if given the chance, I can do anything? I can make sense."

My anxiety continued to get worse and I had to be perfect to feel normal, to feel whole. I needed the thumbs up or the high five or the

"Way to go!" to feel I belonged or fit in. I needed to hear "I love you", "I appreciate you", "you did a good job, Karen", and, "I need you". If I didn't have that approval, I would feel low about myself and wonder why I wasn't good enough.

I allowed these worries to consume me and to dictate who I was as a person. I allowed people's actions towards me validate who I truly was. If they teased me or made a silly joke just to poke fun at me or if they ignored me, I was anxious that the statements were true and I would feel lesser than. I would feel stupid and if I was ignored I felt insignificant and worried that I was forgotten. It didn't matter what I thought of myself; it mattered what they thought of me... or what I thought they thought of me. My perception was often a misunderstanding or an illusion. I often worried, anxiously jumped to conclusions and felt unworthy. During this time of my life, this anxiety was my 'normal.'

One day, after I came across some hidden information, I confronted my spouse about his interactions and inappropriate behavior with other women. This topic of other women always brought me so much anxiety. I had many mixed emotions. One, I was hurt; two, I was confused and three; I was angry which brought on feelings of intense anxiety. I was becoming shaky. I trembled. Mentally, I was in a state of chaos. I always felt lost, worried and really stupid that I was left in the dark about this stuff. How could this happen to me without me noticing? I always thought of myself as quite sharp, but now I questioned my intelligence and questioned my ability to focus. I felt lesser than. I would constantly ask myself, "Why is this happening in my marriage and why can't I control this situation?" I would go into an obsession to find out answers. "Who was this woman this time? When did this happen? What's her name?" Then I would obsessively dig for more information, staying awake all night searching, but deep inside I felt more pain as more was revealed to me. The mix of emotions was incredibly toxic, yet I continued this dark path of anxiety and unhealthy behaviour. "Ah ha! Here's her phone number, I found it! Should I call? No, forget it. I will just send her a polite message on Facebook kindly asking her to stay away from my marriage. Yes, that's better, classier. I gotta stay classy. I don't want to look like an angry, crazy wife. Stay calm Karen, don't let them see you weak." I would write to these women and feel a sense of accomplishment, then I would go for a drive to clear my head. As I drove, feelings of failure would return, "Damn it, how did I miss these damn details. I'm so blind, stupid, so flippin' dumb. How did I let this get by me?" I would bang my head on the steering wheel and yell, "What did I do wrong? I'm such an idiot. Why is this happening to me again?" I would stay up night after night trying to put more pieces together and continue to obsess with these mysteries. I would use all my energy to investigate details so that I had more 'control' of the situation. I was sick and tired of living in the unknown. I felt so much anxiety about being in the dark. If I could just find out more clues, more answers, then I believed I could be free of fear of the unknown.

One time, I saw emails from another woman who I didn't know. She wrote about the time they spent together during his business trip-this again became another heated conversation between him and I. So, I walked away from the kitchen where we were both arguing, and I went up to the bedroom ensuite to be alone. He went downstairs in the basement to join the boys. I tried to deal with my feelings of betrayal; however, I wasn't able to process my feelings logically. In- stead, racing thoughts of inadequacy and unworthiness consumed me. I closed the door shut and locked it to ensure my family wouldn't hear me breaking down. I began to have a shortness of breath, and my throat tightened up. I was having a serious panic attack! I felt so dizzy. I got in the shower to cool off and tried to be still. I got on my hands and knees in the tub with the water running down my back. Leaning my forehead on the cold ceramic, I screamed, "I hate my life!" Despair and unexplainable fear spun through my mind; my brain was in pandemonium overdrive. I grabbed my hair with both hands and screamed, "I'm not good enough! I'm not perfect enough! Why am I here? Who loves me?" A surge of anxiety raced through my veins. I scratched my skin until it bled, and I cried until I couldn't cry anymore. I was so angry with myself for not being able to manage my emotions. My childhood feelings of inadequacy were resurfacing, and my mental struggle was intensifying. It felt as though it was forever before the panic attack finally began to diminish- I felt depleted. I didn't want to say goodnight to my husband or children who were still in the basement two floors beneath me the entire time. I just slipped into my bed and stared at the ceiling. I was numb and now emotionless and just wanted to sleep. I hoped that when I woke up, I would feel better.

I was on an anxiety high every day and couldn't get off the roller coaster ride. I battled with this mental war for years about our relationship, the other women, my stresses at work, his stresses at work, our finances and of course, the heavy baggage I brought into the marriage from my childhood. I tried to deal with my anxiety all while trying to maintain the illusion that I was ok and that I could manage as an employee, a mother, a wife, a friend and be a strong person overall. I continued to live in fear. The fear of not being good enough. The fear of never being loved or validated. My mind was constantly in disarray and turmoil. I took several extra strength Advil a day to decrease my migraines and I rarely slept. I lost over 30 pounds, I suffered from major digestion issues and my hair was falling out due to alopecia (a medical hair-loss condition which affected my scalp.) My sweat glands were surgically removed because I would sweat profusely from anxiety. I had cold tingling hands and feet, shortness of breath, constant muscle tension in my back and an inability to be still or calm. It got so bad, that at times, I had no clue what I was even worried about. I would draw a blank and lose my memory about what was worrying me. I no longer recalled the reason, yet I still felt anxious. It was now becoming just an everyday habitual feeling that I couldn't shake off. It was frustrating to live with, and it interfered with my communication. I had trouble getting my thoughts out, and I stuttered on my words. I spoke in circles and my heart would race. I was a mess!

My thoughts were like clouds floating in my mind, each a different shade of grey. I was completely incapable of tolerating any type of uncertainty; I knew that I needed to seek out help.

On one particularly stressful day, I had another severe panic attack while I was at home. Once I calmed down, I got in my car and drove, then sat in the parking lot of my family doctor's office for over an hour just gripping the steering wheel. I took a deep breath and finally got the courage to walk in. I slowly opened my mouth and whispered to the receptionist, "I need help. I'm not feeling well. I really need some help." This was my first step to recovery...

I was referred to a psychologist and was diagnosed with General Anxiety Disorder (GAD), a mental illness with symptoms of excessive worry, uneasiness and dread for a long period of time.

People who suffer from anxiety often worry intensely about health, relationships, family issues, finances, and work, and this worry interferes with daily life. I was also diagnosed with Dermatillomania, a form of OCD which is the repetitive picking at one's own skin to the extent of causing severe damage and scars. This was a symptom and response to my anxiety; I would scratch and pick until my skin bled. I felt like an ugly monster. I couldn't look at myself in the mirror. The psychologist placed me on sick leave from work for several months, and I was admitted to daily group rehabilitation sessions at the hospital for recovery. I didn't tell many people, just a few friends, because I felt really embarrassed that I needed help with my mental health. (There's a stigma that one is weak if one can't cope on one's own, which is now getting better because community initiatives are spreading awareness).

I had attended daily and participated in Cognitive-Behavioral Therapy (CBT), which helps people to develop strategies for becoming and staying healthy. The goal of CBT was to prepare me to take a more active, positive, and responsible role in my life regarding to my thoughts, emotions and responses to challenges, and to be able to respond to setbacks in a healthier and more productive manner. We did morning meditations and breathing exercises, we had group therapy lead by the onsite psychologist, and we went for daily group walks, we did yoga, and we took cooking classes to learn how to make healthy meals. There was homework daily (the workbook was so thick, and it required a lot of hard effort and soul searching to complete it). I really had to dig deep and be vulnerable when answering the workbook questions. A lot came up to the surface during my days in rehabilitation therapy. I left there learning how to identify negative thoughts and emotions, how to cope with grief and loss and how to overcome my sleep disorders. I learned the necessary skills to resolve relationship difficulties with others and most importantly with myself. I was able to better deal with my social anxiety, my self–esteem was strong and my self- care became a priority. Rehabilitation therapy was a long, tough road, but, by the grace of God, commitment and determination, I pushed through. A brighter ray of hope beamed in my life. I was on my way to creating the life I wanted. A fresh start.

Life Lesson #5:

Don't believe everything you think. That which consumes your mind, controls your life. Self-care is not a reward, it's a requirement. Make your health, mind body and soul a priority.

Is there a physical, mental, emotional, or spiritual health issue in your life that you have been neglecting? Write it below. Acknowledge it, seek help and get support.

_____

_____

_____

_____

_____

_____

_____

_____

_____

_____

_____

_____

_____

_____

Affirmations for Health

42. This is only temporary. Smile, breathe, and go slowly. Every breath I inhale calms me, and every breath I exhale takes away tension.
43. I am not my thoughts and feelings, and they don't have to bring me down.
44. I am conquering this illness; I am defeating it steadily each day.
45. I release fear and replace it with power, love, and a sound mind.
46. I believe in my ability to refrain from addictions that are not healthy for me.
47. Every cell in my body vibrates with energy and health. I am completely pain free.
48. With every outward breath, I release stress from my body.
49. I am surrounded by people who encourage and sup- port healthy choices.
50. I won't let my fear of what could happen make nothing happen.

Chapter 6-
The Freedom Dove

I was released from rehabilitation, and I continued to see a therapist for follow up sessions because although I did a lot of recovery work, my ten-year marriage continued to be rocky. The conflict with other women continued, finances were still very tight, (we had to refinance our home), my personal issues from my childhood of inadequacy and self-doubt were beginning to resurface, and I allowed them to spill over into my marriage. We tried marriage counselling, but things still weren't working out. I began to have major setbacks that contributed towards the marital tensions because I wasn't managing my emotions well. I was sensitive, irritable, and paranoid and this was affecting the relationship. I too contributed to the breakdown of the marriage. I was becoming 'checked out'. I ignored these red flags and tried to remain optimistic. Deep inside, I hoped the issues in our marriage would repair themselves.

My husband and I booked an island getaway to celebrate our ten-year wedding anniversary. I had hoped it would be magical and full of bliss and rekindle a spark. Instead, the trip was a nightmare. On the second night of the trip, we were in our resort hotel room and my husband was taking a shower to get ready for us to go out to a nice dinner, but something in my heart didn't feel right. I didn't feel completely connected to him, something was just off. So, I asked God for a sign, a sign to help me put my mind at ease. I started to get into an anxious state because the familiar feelings of the fear of the unknown within my marriage and the "uh oh something is terribly wrong again" feeling crept inside my head. So, I went into action and started looking for answers. Finally, something just came over me, and I a decided to look inside his wallet. I found a letter he had hand written which had expressed his emotions to another woman... I was humiliated. I confronted him when he got out of the shower, but it was a blur. I could hear his voice vaguely, but my mind was elsewhere. My heart was elsewhere. I needed to distance myself from the pain. I slowly left the room, went into the hotel elevator, and I walked towards the front desk reception area. I felt like all eyes were on me and as though everyone in the lobby knew what just happened to my marriage. As people and families were checking in at the front desk and coming and going with their suitcases and fruity, colorful margaritas in their hands, they were laughing and having a wonderful time. I looked down at the floor in embarrassment, and I felt like I was a nobody amongst a lot of somebodies. I just heard a buzz of people hustling back and forth with beach towels and sunscreen, holding hands and felt like I wasn't even alive, like I was invisible. I just saw happiness everywhere, and truly, I felt like a loser, like a failure, like a woman who just can't succeed at anything. My face was flushed, and tears rolled down my cheeks. I thought to myself, "Get me outta here, I just wanna go home."

I walked towards the private beach and my heart broke as I watched everything crumble around me. The whole island experience felt like I was watching a horrible movie. It was as if I was standing there watching my own life melting and slipping away in front of me. It was as if I was looking at an image of myself laying there in the sand at the shoreline slowly dying. It was surreal. I remember standing there and hoping the ghost- like woman, (who was the old me) would just wake up! I tried yelling at the old me, but the old Karen Carrington could no longer hear me. As the waves drew closer to the shoreline, she was pulled away into the sea, and she slowly slipped below the water. I couldn't save her. She died there. The old Karen Carrington stayed there on that island and drowned.

Now, looking back, I believe God allowed that to happen because He wanted me to find the new Karen Carrington. Sometimes things have to come to an end to make room for better things to begin. I cried on that island as I laid on the sand and looked up at the sky, tears in my eyes and not one face of familiarity to comfort me. I closed my eyes and heard my own heart beating slowly in my chest. It was odd; the pattern sounded different, it was unique. It had a rhythm to it, like it was trying to send me a message. Something new was happening, like a rebirth. I cried out to God, "This is not my destiny. I know you have a better plan for my life." I flew back to Toronto, and I filed for divorce the following Monday.

"In the end, she became more than what she expected. She became the journey, and like all journeys, she did not end, she just simply changed directions and kept going." R.M, Drake

I acquired a lawyer who took care of all the details. I was vulnerable with her and allowed her to guide me through this overwhelming process. For the first time in a long time, I felt cared for. I let go of the need to solve my marriage issues and trusted the process. However, I was still feeling embarrassed inside that my marriage had failed. I avoided my old church and stayed away from social events because I didn't want to talk about my situation to anyone. But occasionally, I would bump into old acquaintances. When I saw them, I wanted to run! My body would freeze, and my mind went into overdrive.

"Aw man, shoot, here they come! They're going to ask me how I am. I need to hide! Where's the exit? Where's a washroom? OMG, get me outta here! Help!" My heart would race as they approached me. Each second felt like slow motion. 5...4...3...2...1... Shoot! Eye contact would be made, and the awkward conversation would begin.

"Hi Karen! Long time no see. You look great! How are the boys? Where's hubby? I haven't seen you around. Is everything ok?" I would quickly manage to change the subject until the awkward encounter was over. "God, I can't do this. I feel like a failure. I'm a divorced, single mother, and this really sucks."

But, on the bright side, even though the divorce was rough on my family, we managed to keep everything quite amicable for the boys' sake. It wasn't a messy warzone battlefield; no blood was shed. There were a few ups and downs of course, ill feelings and pain, yes, but it was an over all civil process.

It was a sad time for all of us because our family was torn apart. It was hard to accept and brought a lot of pain. But because the marriage was continuously unhealthy and strained (yes, there were some happy moments of course), but for me, the bad outweighed the good. The trust was broken for the last time and for myself and my boys, I believed it was the best decision I could have made. Although we didn't work out as husband and wife, my ex-husband is an excellent father and a fair person. He always steps up to the plate and takes care of his responsibilities. He remains active in the boys' lives, pays child support on time, and openly and politely communicates with me when arranging pick up and drop off times for our younger son. And for these reasons, I respect him.

A few months after the divorce, I wanted to make myself feel better, and online dating seemed like a quick fix to fill the void and ease the pain of loneliness. I logged onto these dating sites that my girlfriend at the gym told me about. It was super exciting! So many new faces to choose from! I began to fill out my diva profile and upload a nice photo. Nothing too racy, professional, or boring and added a brief description of myself. Joining these sites brought up some insecurities. It was all so new to me.

I clicked away at the keyboard and began to enter my personal information in the boxes and continued to complete my profile. It was going well until it asked me for my status. This was the first time I had to write the word divorced. I slowly typed each letter one by one. D.I.V.O.R.C.E.D. I stared at the monitor as tears flowed down my cheeks. There it was in black and white. My new status, my new label. I closed my eyes and slowly exhaled. I wanted this to all be a bad dream, but it was my new reality. I wanted to hide under my blankets. I can remember telling myself that maybe I don't deserve joy. I prayed to God to give me the strength to shift out of that thought pattern. I wanted to put myself out there to see what could happen.

The New Karen Carrington is a firm believer in going for what she deserves and nothing less. I wasn't looking for a new husband nor a long-term relationship, but I was looking for companionship. I needed to work on myself, but I also wanted to make new friends. I wanted to focus on rebuilding my life, so I knew that one-night stands and emotionless relationships were not the answer.

I looked at my final profile and was excited for this new adventure. I began to date and really enjoyed meeting new people. I met some great men online, and it was fun picking out new outfits and looking nice for these dates. I was feeling like me, again. Some dates included candle-light dinners, movies, and walks by the water front (which were my favorite). I got to see what I liked and disliked in men and because I hadn't dated in years, it was exciting to connect with new personalities and see what was out there. I met some really refined gentleman. Some dates went really well, and I made some really good like-minded friends. I remember laughing so hard with one guy I dated that I banged the restaurant dinner table and held my belly as I burst out laughing. Oh man! He seriously had the best stories. He would recite these stories really loud in the restaurant; he was so expressive! Those were some good times man! I'm still laughing at this guy's jokes as I write. I will say, however, dating wasn't always a bed of roses. Listen! Hear me when I say some of these dates were absolutely terrible and OMG some even freakin' traumatizing. Lord have mercy, that's for another book, trust me!

Anyways, I realized that I needed to work on all areas of my life, so in addition to the dating site, I signed up for local meet up groups, women empowerment events, church gatherings and networking mixers in my area. Wow! I have met some truly amazing people along the way and made genuine, lasting friendships. I went out of my comfort zone, and who would have known how far that would take me? It's important to remember that coming out of our comfort zone and taking a leap of faith is really tough in the beginning but stepping out of our comfort zone is where the real growth happens.

I released the shame of being divorced, and finally I felt free of judgement. I let go of the taboo of being 'a divorced woman' that I felt. I was liberated to express how I felt, so liberated that I got another tattoo on my left wrist (a very visible place where I could see it). It is of a dove which symbolizes freedom. Although I was divorced, with one door closed, new doors were opening for me. I met so many wonderful, new, like-minded people and friends. It was a whole, new exciting world for me! Remember, you can create the life you want; it's up to you to see the good in everything. It's up to you to shift your mindset.

Life Lesson #6:

Sometimes, not getting what you want and what you think you need is the biggest blessing of all. Love the idea of loving yourself instead of the idea of someone else loving you.

Are you in a relationship, friendship or family tie that no longer serves you or the other person in a healthy way? Write their name(s) below and pray or meditate about it. Ask yourself if it's best to continue the relationship or to part ways.

_____

_____

_____

_____

_____

_____

_____

_____

_____

Affirmations for Recovering from a Broken Relationship

52. I will resist the urge to contact someone that is in my past and that should not be in my present.

53. It is what it is. I accept it. I forgive myself for my faults and my mistakes, and I am willing to move on.

54. No matter how I feel, I will get up, dress up, show up and never give up.

55. I forgive those who have harmed me in my past, and I will not have thoughts of revenge. I will peacefully forgive.

56. My ability to conquer my challenges is limitless; my potential to succeed is infinite.

57. Many people look up to me and recognize my worth; I am valued. It's their loss if they don't see it.

58. I acknowledge my own self-worth; my confidence is soaring.

59. I am able to take space for myself when needed.

60. I can respectfully communicate my feelings.

61. Having a healthy relationship is extremely important to me. I will part ways if it no longer serves me.

Chapter 7-
The River Cleanse

My divorce was finalized. We sold the family home. I bought a new car. I snagged an upscale, 3-bedroom, high-rise condo for me and my two sons and decorated it with modern, sleek furniture. It was a whirlwind, but I was excited to be starting out fresh. I felt on top of the world! That first night, I sat on my leather couch. I felt like a queen on my throne. I don't drink wine, (I know some people wonder how I manage without wine, but I do!) but I was still celebrating the new life I was creating for myself! I wasn't a victim. My mentality had to change, and there was no time to be sad or depressed. I really wanted to celebrate my new life and embrace this new fresh start. I put red, sparkly juice in a wine glass and made a platter of expensive cheese, exotic fruits, artisan crackers and French pastries. I treated myself like royalty. Some nights, if I really wanted to spice it up, I would put on spa music, light some scented candles, wear a fancy leopard print shiny night gown, and spritz on my Beyoncé perfume. Oooh lala. I was a total glam diva. Every time I did this routine, I was on a total high!

One evening, I decided that instead of making the usual royal platter, I would venture out and get some Thai food. I could have ordered in, but I really wasn't good at that! I would ask the agent on the line 10, 000 questions and have them explain to me the promotions and daily specials over and over, again, then I would have to wait 45 minutes for delivery. I always got so confused and impatient! Argggh. Honestly, it's just easier if I go out. Anyways, I had on an amazing black leather outfit with faux fur around my neck and silver stilettos (hey, you never know who you will run into, right?). I slayed in my outfit. I confidently walked towards the Thai restaurant with my blonde hair flowing and lip gloss dazzling and BOOM! The phone call comes in. "Mom, come home quick! The condo is flooded!"

I raced home, flung the door open, and looked around at the damage. Water was gushing everywhere! A pipe in the interior walls had burst and water was flowing at full force. I lost everything. I fell to the floor onto my hands and knees. I stayed there, immersed in water in a helpless position of defeat. I cried for an hour to the security guard who was on site, "How do I fix this damage on my own? Where do I start without help?" I took a mop and tried to get into fix-it mode, but I fell back to the floor. An emergency flood crew came on site within minutes, and I watched them throw out all my new but damaged furniture, clothing and belongings. Now this was a crappy day.

In a matter of minutes, I went from a queen in silver stilettos to a defeated, grungy woman standing in muddy water. Everything was gone. The boys and I had to leave the condo and live somewhere else temporarily. It was such a hassle and inconvenience going back and forth. Eventually, we regained access to our home and lived amongst dust and debris for a very long time because it took months for the contractors to complete the repairs in my suite. I just laid on a mattress and stared at the ceiling most nights. I refused to reach out for help because I didn't want to look like a needy, struggling, single mother who lost everything... yet again.

I continued to handle the paperwork for my divorce and the flood insurance on my own. I went to work every day, smiled and came home like nothing happened. I really wanted to manage this whole issue on my own because I was prideful and embarrassed- I didn't want to ask for assistance. But, then I would look around my house and think, "My God, my new snazzy condo is a damn construction zone." It was a hot mess, and I was resentful, frustrated and overwhelmed. My condo was no longer the comfortable peaceful place that I wanted for my sons. We spent our first holiday season under these rough conditions. I just couldn't make it a nice Christmas for my sons that year. My feelings of failure were at an all time high. I decided to give up on the Christmas festivities and celebrations. My heart just wasn't in to it. I sent the boys to their father's side of the family for Christmas, and I decided to volunteer at a men's shelter downtown Toronto to feed the homeless on Christmas Day. I sent an email, registered to be a server, and spent the day serving meals. I needed to do something that would pull me outside of the slump I was in. Giving back to others always does that for me. Being able to show that love to people who have no where to go on Christmas allowed me to feel selfless and pushed me to actually feel happy for the first time in a long time. It was exactly where I needed to be. I really enjoy giving back and putting a smile on peoples' faces. I love pouring into the lives of others.

A few years later, another flood occurred in my condo. This time it started in the bathroom. Thousands of dollars in damages. SH*T! It was bad. Water flowed everywhere and the hardwood floors were destroyed instantly. I let out a huge sigh as I placed both hands over my face as tears began to flow. I could go through insurance again like the last time, but I refused. I wasn't going to live in that turmoil again so I took a cash advance on my credit cards to repair the destruction. I hired a contractor and within a week, it was 100% completed. Ah- hhhh, relief. I sat on the shiny new floors and looked around at the final stunning product. I reflected on the bible scripture Isaiah 32:18 "God makes a promise to us. He says my people will live in peaceful dwelling places, in secure homes, in undisturbed places of rest." I meditated on that passage all day. I closed my eyes and knew what I had to do. God's word says He provides peace in our home. I opened my eyes and said to my self, "Karen, it's time for a fresh start." Water is symbolic for rejuvenation, cleansing, rebirth, restoration and new beginnings. It was a River Cleanse. It was time to move on. The truth is, I loved that condo. I had been there for years and lived through so much healing in it. But much had changed there, too. My older son moved out and got married, and it was just me and my younger son. I lived there during my divorce; it was my sanctuary, my safe haven. It helped me transform. But, I knew these two floods were a sign to move on.

In life, we need to see the signs and act on them. Although the condo was restored, I knew it was no longer the path for me; I no longer needed to be there. I picked up the phone and gave my landlord notice that I was moving. We had an awesome chat. I told him it was time for me to move on to somewhere new. Man, I really liked that guy, he was always really good to me. Anyway, I sold most of my furniture, packed up my boxes, and was ready for a new life. It was time, again, for a fresh start.

I made the decision to move downtown Toronto in the heart of the city near the iconic CN tower. I always wanted to live right downtown beside the waterfront and see all the festivities and enjoy the view of the monumental tower- Toronto's most recognizable and celebrated structure. The CN Tower is so inspiring! I'm in total awe and feel a sense of pride every time I see it. For me, its vast height symbolizes solid strength and unbreakable-ness. I knew in my heart that that's where I belonged in order to live the life I imagined since I was a teenager. My belief is that we become a product of our environment. So, I immersed myself in this new situation, leaped in faith, landed exactly where I belonged, steps away from the CN tower. Don't be afraid to start again, over and over. It's a chance to rebuild what you want. I have started fresh several times, and each time, I become a little stronger and a little wiser.

"If you're brave enough to say good bye, life will reward you with a new hello." -Paulo Coehlo

Life Lesson #7:

Sometimes, we are taken into troubled waters not to drown, but to be cleansed.

Have you received a sign that it's time to chase your dreams? Write down a dream that you still have yet to accomplish. What has stopped you? Take the courageous step.

_____

_____

_____

_____

_____

_____

_____

_____

_____

_____

_____

_____

_____

_____

Affirmations for Overcoming

62. Though these times are difficult, they are only a short phase of life.

63. I am courageous.

64. I am supported which enables me to be f illed with courage.

65. I am strong.

66. I am supported which enables me to be f illed with strength and face any challenge.

67. I accept help from others in my time of need.

68. Accepting help is a sign of strength.

69. I am willing to try new things and face new chal- lenges in a new direction

70. Solutions come to me on how to solve every chal- lenge or problem that I face.

71. I am capable of solving problems that I face.

Chapter 8-
Love at First Swipe

I was happy with my life and my new journey but quite a bit of debt had ramped up, especially my divorce fees, previous loans and credit card debt. I would swipe my credit card every time an emergency popped up, and I was never prepared for a rainy day. As a teen, I was not given much financial guidance or advice. With all the chaos that went on during my childhood years, financial guidance from my parents just didn't fit into the scene. I didn't have a positive outlook on finances, at all. I am not placing full blame on my parents as I am responsible for my financial habits; however, my initial introduction to money was not a positive one. This behavior of not saving and overspending continued as an adult. I had various loans, and my bank account was often in the red, I mean bright red! This issue crept up on me. I didn't even realize that it was escalating. Seeing these high balances gave me big time anxiety. I accrued so much debt and had so little to show for it, it was depressing.

I often felt like a failure when I went to the bank. I would feel so uncomfortable at the bank teller counter. One time I needed to withdraw money and the bank machines were out of service, so I had to see an agent. I was next in line and the older woman with a bossy miserable voice yelled out, "next!" I approached the counter wondering who on earth peed in her cornflakes that morning. I provided my info for her to open my file and she flatly asked, "How much do you need to withdraw, Ms. Carrington?" I replied, "I don't know my balance, once you let me know, I will decide how much I need to withdraw." She slowly took off her glasses, looked me dead in the eye and said, "Sweetheart, I have never seen such a mess. There's so much activity in this account! I think this is the most withdrawal transactions I have ever seen in my banking career. You owe $60,000. You sure you want to withdraw funds again today?" I was devastated! I thought, "Is she allowed to talk to me like that? Did she just publicly label me as a failure?" I quickly closed my wallet and shot back, "Um hello lady, you're not being professional. Can I see the bank supervisor, please? Trust me, they will vouch for me that I am a long-term customer here and always make my minimum payments on time!" I dealt with this bank for years and I was a star client! Little did I know that I was a star client because I had such a huge debt load with them. The bank supervisor came out and apologized and offered me those free bland looking undecorated cookies they had out on display with a complimentary styrofoam cup of coffee but I declined, I gracefully walked out of the bank thinking, "I don't need this crap, I'll go to another bank location." But deep inside, I knew she was right.

I was so embarrassed. I knew I had to do something because the burden of my finances was causing me so much stress that I couldn't sleep at night.

I would stay up all night and transfer money from one account to another. I had it down to a science. But eventually, the debt was increasing up to my eyeballs. I was starting to feel the pinch when everything was reaching its limit and I was a few dollars away from maxing out.

I became really self-conscious at cash registers. If I was buying groceries, I was worried I would see a huge "DECLINE" sign across the cash register screen. I would swipe my card, hold my breath, look away from the cashier and pray like my life depended on it. "Please God, let this transaction go through. I need these groceries. Please don't let these people behind me see the decline."

I was afraid to give up my credit cards. They were my safety net, and I didn't want to lose my freedom. But, you know what? In actuality, I was losing my mental freedom. I was under the bondage of debt and it was an unhealthy way to live. I was so far into debt; it felt impossible to imagine myself debt free. It was a goal that seemed unreachable. There was a lot of shame and I felt like a failure because no matter how hard I tried to save or pay bills, I could never make ends meet. At the time, I didn't have strong financial planning skills. Something always came up and I wasn't prepared. I was just going in circles. I would take out loans to pay other loans and didn't have a strategic solid plan, just a lot of band aid solutions that were bound to fail.

I needed to get my life back in order. After a few months of research on different options, I came to a solution that would work well for me. I was ready to begin my journey toward financial freedom, and I made the bold, courageous decision to finally make things right in my life. I entered into debt counselling with a reliable company to file a Consumer Proposal, which is an arrangement negotiated with creditors through a Licensed Insolvency Trustee. It's an alternative to filing for bankruptcy. When you file a Consumer Proposal, you agree to pay a portion of what you owe, and your creditors agree to absorb the balance.

The process was emotional, and I had my ups and downs. I realize this option isn't for everybody, but after long deliberation and advice from the credit counsellors, I finally made the choice that was best for me. I was afraid but day by day I took it step by step.

I no longer buy things on credit. Now, I work within my budget and I have money in my savings! It feels great! I always shop with a grocery list, so I won't randomly buy things. I track my spending so that I can monitor my money and where it is going and I save money. Putting money aside for savings was and is essential to staying within the boundaries of my budget. Even if I only put a small amount aside each paycheck, the savings built up quickly. I began being mindful to take out enough cash to last me one week at a time. Using cash was better than continuously swiping a credit card or debit card because I could physically see the money leave my hands. Lastly, I had to look through all my receipts and find expenses to be cut. It took a lot of commitment and dedication, but I stuck to it. I was really happy with my decision to file the consumer proposal. I had a fresh start. Finally! I no longer had to break out into a sweat before I took a swipe.

Financial instability is very stressful. But, when you don't have the weight of debt hanging over you, you get to breathe easier, you live better. It's a fresh start to make things right. Set a budget and stick to it so that you can create the life you want.

Life Lesson # 8:

Sacrifice is empowering. We must make sacrifices to get from where we are to get to where we want to be. With the right approach, commitment, and determination, you can achieve anything you put your mind to.

What sacrifices do you currently need to make in order to reach your financial goals?

_____

_____

_____

_____

_____

_____

_____

_____

_____

_____

Affirmations for Financial Freedom

72. I accept responsibility for the tasks that need to be completed.

73. The more I give without expectation, the more I will receive.

74. I have the ability make sound financial decisions.

75. I am setting good financial examples for my chil- dren and the younger generations.

76. I live within my financial means. I am in control of my f inances.

77. I attract incredible opportunities to increase my wealth and my life.

78. I have financial freedom, and I am financially re- sponsible.

79. I thank God for my financial securities. I attract prosperity easily and use my prosperity to further God's Kingdom.

80. I can do anything I set my mind to starting right now, today.

81. I not only receive money, but I also now give money. I give generously, and I receive graciously.

Chapter 9-
Remove, Release and Reset

Sometimes in life, in order to achieve your goals and reach success, you may have to let go of some of the people from your past. Just because you choose success it doesn't mean your friends or family will. Some of them will always see you for who you were and not for who you are becoming. A few of my close friends felt more comfortable if I continued to be the Karen Carrington I used to be, but I had to move forward without these people.

Over time, as the success in my life began to expand, a few people no longer supported my dreams. I exhausted myself trying to appease them and keep them in my life. As I elevated myself, some friends in my circle became silent and distant. It was such a foreign feeling to me. One good friend of mine, without warning, blocked me from social media and didn't pick up my calls. There was no explanation. She just disappeared. Just poof! Vanished! Years of friendship just gone. At first, I was in shock and thought, "oh, no she didn't!" Then I became confused, which then led to resentment and anger and in the end, I was left with a dull sadness. I had never experienced that before and went through all the emotions of grief and depression. It happened a year later with another friend, and I began to notice a pattern. These people were envious of my success. I reflected on some of the past comments they had made about the things I was doing, and now it all made sense. They were suffering from their own personal emotional issues and they were stuck there. Life had simply moved on. I was moving on and they didn't share my joy.

I was frustrated that I was oblivious that didn't connect the dots. I confided in my mentor and asked for advice on how to rectify the situation. My mentor explained to me that this wasn't an issue that I could control. When someone wants to leave, they will leave. I had to accept that. This even happened when I was dating. Some men saw my independence and said to me that they found it difficult to embrace my success. They pointed out that I was too busy investing in my business, and they felt concerned that there was no room for them in my life. Some even said that they felt like they would be left behind! I was so confused! Don't they want a successful, eager woman? Why is this a bad thing that I want more for my life? For me, if I am with a man that I love and if he is supportive and we are meant to be together then of course I would make room in my life for him! Right? To me it was a no- brainer! One of my dates told me that my success made him anxious. Another said I looked too beautiful and too perfect like a Barbie doll. One older gentleman in his fifties who called himself 'Soul Daddy' wanted me to spend more quality time with him so he suggested that I walk away from my business, quit my full-time job, move in with him and help him garden in his back yard. "Whaaaat???!!! Is he out of his mind??!?" He sounded more like a boring 'Sugar Daddy' than a hip 'Soul Daddy' to me, I'll pass thanks.

This whole success thing really had me puzzled. I would lay in bed and wonder why didn't these particular men or friends want to stay? None of it added up to me. At first, I would not accept that they didn't want to stay and I tried to hold onto some of these relationships. I would try to make it all work, but it just never did. These negative relationships that I was trying to maintain were now strained, awkward, forced and felt fake. I eventually realized that walking away from a toxic relationship had nothing to do with me being weak, instead it was a sign of strength. We walk away once we finally realize our own self-worth and value.

I admit, at first, it was hard to release them. I didn't know 'how' to let go. I didn't want any bad vibes or ill feelings. I didn't want to leave them behind, but I knew these old 'friends' and relationships were holding me back and stunting my growth. This handful of people were not a positive influence in my life and it wasn't healthy for me to try to stay. So, I released them or let them walk away. It hurt me inside, and I felt incredibly sad, but I had to do what was best. The only friends you want to keep around you are the ones who fully support you along the way and believe you will reach your dreams.

As time went on, as I began to have more self-confidence and became more aware, I began to quickly identify negative people. I was fully aware if they had a negative vibration or if they exuded low frequencies. I distanced myself from negative people by not answering their calls. I removed them from my phone contact list, I did not reply to their text messages and stopped interacting with them on social media. This took some time, and yes, it sometimes hurt. The truth is I didn't have anger or malice towards them, but eventually I realized that people can stay in our hearts, but they cannot always stay in our lives. The ties had to be broken.

In order to be successful and maintain your inner peace, you need to beware of these people. I'm sure you have come across some of these characters. You know the ones I'm talking about. They complain, they gossip, and they hold grudges forever! Then there's the narcissists who put down others. Oh, and let's not forget the victims, watch out for them! They can be energy vampires and suck the total life out of you if you're not careful. They never ever have a solution to problems and keep coming to you for endless advice that they don't take. If you're not careful, you may absorb these negative energies into your spirit if you allow them in your space for too long. You need to create healthy boundaries by minimizing contact or ignoring them altogether.

In the Bible, Ecclesiastes 3 says, "There's a time for everything and a season for every activity under the heavens. A time to plant and a time to uproot, a time to tear down and a time to build, a time to weep and a time to laugh, a time to embrace and a time to refrain from embracing, a time to search and a time to give up, a time to keep and a time to throw away, a time to tear and a time to mend." This Bible passage helped me see that there is a season for everything, relationships have a life cycle, some shorter than others. And that's okay. Each relationship and friendship serves as a purpose in our lives and we learn from each of them. And you know what!? When God helped me identify and remove these people from my life, it made room for more blessings. I removed myself, released negative people and reset my life. That's the key to moving forward. Remove, Release and Reset. Remember, our destiny is never tied to anyone or anything that has parted from us. We will always have the right people at the right time in our lives if we just pay attention to the signs!

Don't surround yourself with people who bring you down. Elevate yourself and do you! Learn to rejoice in the end of toxic relationships and friendships. Letting someone go doesn't mean you don't care about them anymore, in fact, walking away is actually a step forward for both of you. Take the time to examine your relationships, friendships, and business partnerships carefully. I guarantee you that when you finally find the courage to let go of what doesn't serve you, it will be one of the most rewarding, most freeing practices in your life. Make this your best year ever. YOU are good enough just as you are and there's no need to change for others' approval or validation. Don't adjust yourself to make others comfortable. Don't dull your shine! Create the life you want by letting go and moving forward.

Life Lesson #9:

Letting go is an act of bravery. Letting go of toxic people is a step toward loving yourself.

It can be hard to end a toxic relationship; therefore, you need to get a clear vision of why you are ending it. Do you have a toxic person in your life? Write down how this person or people make you feel and the benefits of ending the toxic relationship.

_____

_____

_____

_____

Affirmations for Letting G

82. I let go of past relationships and clear my spirit of unhealthy chains.

83. I make room for new relationships to enter my life.

84. I am starting life over again.

85. I release what no longer serves me.

86. I see the beauty and significance in starting over.

87. I dare to walk away from all of the familiar relationships that give me a temporary but unsatisfactory sense of self.

88. Letting go does not mean giving up.

89. I am okay to move on.

90. I am a loveable person.

91. Today, I will only look forward not back.

Chapter 10-
Getting Down to Business

I did everything possible to turn my vision of having my own business into a reality. My mission was to create a platform bringing communities together to speak to the masses and inspiring and empowering people to reach their true potential. I enjoy helping people enhance their lives, and I knew that this was my purpose. I worked 9-5 in a corporate office for over 12 years which I enjoy very much even till today (it helps to sculpt and teach me organizational, leadership and communication skills.) After work, I would go home and create in the evening and weekends while having to balance being a single mother. Although at times it was exhausting, and I wanted to give up, I kept on dreaming and creating until I finally launched my business, Karen Carrington Inc. I branded myself by displaying my different artistic talents which encompass 4 main streams. I will explain my business and the profiles more in depth, but first I want to give you some history on why I named it after myself- it's extremely symbolic to my business and personal journey. The elegance of 'Karen Carrington'. I always loved my first name and my former marriage surname paired together. I felt empowered by its glamourous tone. I kept my last name after my divorce because although I wanted to leave the past behind, I was a new woman now, and I knew my full name Karen Carrington had a beautiful ring to it (it had to be part of my vision in some way shape or form!) To take you back a bit, almost every time I introduced myself to someone, they replied with "Ohhhh, Karen Carrington! I love that name; it kinda reminds me the famous TV show "Dynasty!" (a soap opera from the 1980s). I heard this comment so often that one day I felt compelled to research the history of the show more in depth. I came across an online entry written by the show's co-executive producer, Esther Shapiro. My jaw literally dropped as I read through it. The words she wrote described me to a T. She said "The women of Dynasty were extraordinarily beautiful and always wore the prettiest clothes imaginable. They were not doormats for men to use, and they were never victims. These women of Dynasty lived their lives with purpose; they were passionate, engaged competitively in business, and were strong and goal-oriented". I screamed "OMG! That's me!" It went on to further explain one of the main characters, Alexis Carrington, who exudes an aura of sensuality and sophistication was a fearless, intelligent, jetsetter, an independent dynamo who simply never settled for anything but the very best, a world class woman who was in total control of her life, who never went anywhere without being the center of attention. She was a creative artist and branded everything she touched with her distinctive signature. I was in awe when I came across this article. I completely identified with this character, and it was at that moment when I received 100% confirmation that I made the right choice to name my business after myself. (In fact, if the show ever reruns, I'm auditioning for sure! I would totally fit right in!)

Anyway, I continued to build my business by branding myself and as I previously mentioned, it has 4 main streams. The first is my talk show, "The Karen Carrington Show", which is based on healthy relationships, emotional intelligence, mental wellness and healthy life balance. It is very successful and has viewers of all ages, male and female; people of all walks of life tune in from all over the world. I am proud of how it has blessed many lives. I receive so many emails and messages on social media about how the show has touched people, and this truly warms my heart! The second stream is my facilitated workshops which I deliver as a Certified Trainer, and they're based on self-care, self-love, mindfulness and personal growth. I've facilitated these workshops in Toronto and as far as California. The third stream is being an author. My writing helps readers create the life they want. And, the fourth stream is being an Inspirational Speaker and Event Host which inspires and uplifts the masses through speaking on stage. I branded my business based on my mission statement which is "To continuously make special connections and deliver an empowering message to people leaving them inspired, encouraged and feeling loved."

As my business grew, I was constantly meeting new people through networking and traveling. To me, traveling and networking were essential to the foundation and growth of my business because the experiences and connections I made helped me gather impactful content through these real-life adventures. I would learn so much by listening to random strangers' stories in airports, on the beach, hotel lobbies, and in Uber rides. Oh, the things I would hear! Life changing! Everything from near death experiences or people leaving their home country to start a new life to a woman fearing her future because she was about to press harassment charges against her boss. I empathetically listened to their life experiences and although I didn't know their full names or identity, I felt emotionally connected to them. I would find the life lessons in their journeys and kept a piece of each of these stories with me as I moved forward. I'm like a journalist. I would take their stories and piece them along with my own life experiences and create content for my talk show, workshops and speaking engagements. I never received a university degree, but the degree I did receive was from the "School of Life and the Lives of Others" and from there I became an official "Creative Communication Artist". These extraordinary stories from extraordinary people, including myself, have been the foundation of Karen Carrington Inc.

In addition to meeting new people, a lot of my inspiration for building a successful business was from my role model, world famous talk show host, actress, producer, and philanthropist, Oprah

Winfrey. She has truly inspired me during my journey through her uplifting powerful messages, business ethic and positive attitude. She is a powerhouse business woman who possesses a wealth of wisdom. She has infamous quotes that I keep in my journal and re-read over and over, again. One of my favorite quotes is, "Surround yourself with only people who are going to lift you higher." This quote was pivotal to my business because it was important that I surrounded myself with uplifting friends when as I was trying to reach new goals. These particular groups of friends are called your "inner circle". These people help you to think through issues and evaluate options. They are the first people to call you out when you are wrong because they truly care for you. They are the people who cheer you up and whose shoulder you can lean on when you are feeling down. When you lose your confidence, they remind you of your amazing capabilities and qualities!

For me personally, I always ensure I have like-minded people in my inner circle. I only have a few people in my close inner circle especially when it comes to getting down to business. Many of my friends that I have met at networking events mean a lot to me and these relationships are fundamental to my business ventures because we are often on the same page and we connect. I enjoy spending time with them, going out to dinner or meeting up to watch a movie together.

Within my inner circle of close friends, I have very few people that I consider my confidants. Confidants are people that you can open up to and be vulnerable with and they are closely intertwined into your life. They are there to make sure you reach your destiny and they help you to dream big! They support you and love you unconditionally. Confidants are those people who are right there beside you. No matter what, they are right there.

One of my confidants is one of my very best friends ever. He pushes me to higher levels, and he has deep insight when I need clarity within my business. He always picks up the phone when I have a new business-oriented vision I need to carry out, he never judges me, and he believes in my ventures. He celebrates me when I succeed and gives me advice when I fail. This guy calls me each morning before 7:00 a.m. and his stern tone in his voice projects directly through my cell phone. All I can hear is this militant-style American accent booming in my ear, "Good mornin', good mornin', good mornin', wake up, wake up, wake up". Then he goes on to explain that "those who sleep miss out!" Then he busts out in a laugh as I reply, "yo, I'm awake, I'm awake, I'm awake, you know me, I'm always working, you know me, I'm never sleeping, always slaying". This is how we open our call each morning and each time it makes me laugh so hard even though it's the same sentence each morning! He was in the military for 8 years in the U.S. and I believe that's why he is so disciplined and dedicated even until today. We speak absolutely everyday about everything in our business. Our business is our passion, and we energize each other. We give each other advice, and we push each other and motivate each other to be the best version of ourselves that we can be. We help each other build an unshakable faith in God and in our dreams. I put everything by my confidant because he tells it like it is!!! He is a no B.S straight shooter, extremely logical, solution-oriented, and always executes with brilliance.

The second confidant of mine means so much to me. He has taught me how to love in ways I never thought possible. He truly believes in me and continuously reminds me of my accomplishments and my potential. He's a visionary philosopher kind of guy who is extremely intellectual and has helped me shift my mindset and expand my thought processes. He's also shown me how to connect with my subconscious and how to bring that awareness to the forefront. He has guided me in daily meditations, helped me redirect any negative energy to a place of love and prosperity and has shown me how to look at different life events in ways I never saw them before. He never judges me, he accepts me for who I am, and this guy is so damn down to earth. He too is a no B.S straight shooter, and we lift and shift one another when we need a boost or push in the right direction when it comes to getting down to business or life lessons. He has such a good heart and is a humanitarian. He encouraged me in the infancy stages of my community outreach work and has helped me realize that I have the ability within me to manifest positive outcomes in my business and my life overall.

A very special close person in my inner circle is my younger son. He is my exclusive travel partner and official business consultant.

He attends conferences with me, he has a keen business sense, he is extremely savvy and like my other confidants, my son is a no nonsense kind of guy. When I'm indecisive about something, I ask him for business advice on any particular subject from the color of my website, the font of a poster, what flight we should take on a trip to what dress I should wear to an event I'm hosting. He answers me once, and if I try to get him to change his mind or persuade him to rethink his response, he gives me this look like, "Lady, I told you once, and I ain't tellin' you again!"

So, needless to say, this kid stays at my right hand at all times. For his 14th birthday, I made a slideshow of memorable pictures and I posted this tribute to my son on social media that went viral. It was my most impactful post with the most likes, reactions and traffic to date and made waves because it demonstrated his astounding character. Without him, my business or my success would not be where it is today.

"I was devastated. 6 years ago I was divorced and alone. My world shattered and was completely different as I once knew it. I had to learn to rebuild my entire life through the pain. My heart died, my soul was empty. But you my son, you were there. You stayed so strong for mommy. We became best friends. We learned to survive as one. You slept beside me. You traveled with me. You trusted the process. You trusted me and never doubted me. You gave me advice, held my hand and supported me. Our identical humour kept me going. You just got me. Son, you understood me. My jokes, my quirkiness. You never judged me. You took away all the confusion and kept it real when I couldn't see clearly. When my feelings got in the way, your logic set me straight. You taught me to love like I've never loved before and that life is truly worth it. I am a stronger woman because of you. as you enter another stage in your life today, may God guide you to bless others the way you have blessed me. Happy 14th birthday son."

I still get teary-eyed every time I read that. My sons mean the world to me, they are the reason why I do the things that I do, they are the reason I work so hard. I want to leave behind a legacy for them.

If you have special confidants in your lifetime, you are truly blessed. They are your soul mate kind of friends. These people are the ones you tell your dreams to. They will tell you when you are right and correct you when you are wrong. They are with you, and they are there to make sure you reach your goals and your destiny. They are the ones who support your dreams 100%, and respect your dreams 100% because they love you. When you're happy, they're happy for you. When you ask if they are ready to rock and roll and ride or die with you, they immediately reply "yeah, you know I gotchu".

As I said, my son is my exclusive travel partner. We travelled to Las Vegas after my divorce to attend a conference that helped motivate attendees to start their own businesses. We were really pumped! We knew becoming an entrepreneur was the right choice for me, and my son would be my consultant. From there we continued to travel, experienced new things, and attended more motivational conferences and seminars. One of the key fundamentals that we were taught in these conferences is that the words we speak into the universe manifest into a reality. "If you want it, speak it." During our travel experiences, we have picked up and gone to New York City running into famous pop star, Justin Bieber! He was practicing his performance outside Rockefeller Center, and we ended up being on the Morning Show front row. Another time, we went to Los Angeles and randomly saw talk show host, Ellen DeGeneres on her bike as we waved a warm hello. I met Bishop T.D. Jakes, an inspiring, faith-based influencer in business. He was a featured speaker at the inauguration of Barack Obama. I met Eric Thomas, a famous motivational speaker, Margaret Trudeau, the Prime Minister of Canada- Justin Trudeau's mother. I have also met Marci Ien, Co host of the Social at CTV, Jeanne Beker, Canadian television personality and fashion editor, David Chilton, a Canadian author, investor and television personality; he starred on the famous show Dragon's Den sharing his financial expertise and had the privilege of eating delicacy desserts and munching on appetizers while chatting with the Mayor of Pickering Ontario at a social gathering. I made sure and snapped a photo with each of these aforementioned amazing people to remember the special moments! My son and I once went to a Drake concert, a famous Canadian rapper, and sat in our back-row, cheap seats. I said to myself, "we deserve to be closer to the stage." Moments later, a security guard approached us and escorted us to the front row. It was a surreal experience. Another time, a camera man once spotted me at a fund-raising event and asked me to speak on television about the mental health event they were covering. I shared my personal experience dealing with General Anxiety Disorder, and boom, there I was featured on the 6:00 news.

The reason why am I sharing these encounters is not to boast or brag, rather to show that I spoke each one of these encounters into the universe before they occurred. Our words and thoughts are extremely powerful. I prayed each time before each of these events came to reality. I prayed to God to lead me up to the big stage or behind stage, on set or to shake hands. I lived by faith and set the intention for these encounters to manifest and turn into a reality. Every time I said to myself, "I will meet someone influential on this trip. I will be on that stage today. I know today, good things will happen. I will meet someone famous in the very near future." Then, bam, there I was, either sitting next to these people chatting, picking their brains about how they succeeded and how they created the life they have. Today, I am surrounded by so many wonderful, inspiring, like-minded friends, mentors, fellow entrepreneurs, business men and women, and so many people who share love and joy with me. I receive it and no longer feel unworthy or unlovable as I once did.

Another role model I look up to is author, Jack Canfield. He's an inspiring, motivational speaker, seminar leader, corporate trainer and entrepreneur. His messages inspired me to want more for myself and pushed me to chase my ambitions. His training sessions taught me how to increase my confidence. I began to effectively meditate, I made vison boards and I learned how to live with passion and purpose. Booking my trip to attend his live Break Through to Success Training session in Arizona, was one of the best life choices I have ever made. I am proud I made the brave decision to work towards becoming an official Canfield Certified Trainer.

I am proud of many of the decisions I made because they've made me stronger through the process, the ups and downs, the failures and achievements. I no longer fear my father, nor do I seek his approval. I have forgiven him and found closure through this journey. I have healed from my childhood, and I am now able to help others heal by sharing my story of overcoming. I live the purposeful life I was meant to have.

Life Lesson #10:

Failure is a learning opportunity. Go forth and seize the moment- this is the path of self-improvement. New beginnings are the spaces of growth, fresh starts and possibilities. It is in this precious space where beautiful breakthroughs manifest, and you can create the life you want.

What achievements and goals do you aspire to reach this year in your workplace, your career or your business?

_____

_____

_____

_____

_____

_____

_____

_____

_____

_____

_____

_____

_____

Affirmations for Your Career or Business

92. My efforts are supported by the Universe.

93. My dreams manifest into reality right before my eyes.

94. I am aware that all I need is within me.

95. I live my life without limits and I can do anything I set my mind to.

96. I do the work to achieve my results.

97. I choose to take high-risks to enjoy the high-rewards.

98. I take calculated risks to grow my profitable business.

99. I step out of my comfort zone to ask for the sale.

100. I write down my goals and how I am going to achieve them.

101. I give myself permission to start living my future now.

Chapter 11-
Living a Life of Purpose

There was a point in my life when bright lights would flash in my face and everywhere I turned there would be a new sign pointing in the direction of me stepping into my purpose. Eventually, I knew inside my heart it was time to be the woman God designed me to be. I could no longer ignore the signs because I was denying myself the life that I deserved to live. I always had a burning sensation to have my own talk show and to be an empowering inspirational speaker. I wanted to speak my truth to the masses, to uplift, to inspire and captivate the audience, to bring healing to people who were hurting and energize those who had lost hope. It was always very natural for me to connect with others using my voice of influence. Oprah Winfrey once said during her acceptance speech after she was awarded the Cecil B. DeMille Award for Lifetime Achievement at the Golden Globes, "What I know for sure is that speaking your truth is one of the most powerful tools we all have." I resonated with this quote because it's a reminder that once we unleash our authentic self and share our inner stories with vulnerability, only then are we able to heal and bring healing to others. When we speak our truth, our story is no longer our fortress, instead, it has now transformed into our fuel.

Each time, seconds before the camera is about to roll to kick off my talk show or when I walk on a stage to speak to an audience, I grab hold of the microphone and feel a rush of excitement, passion and adrenaline running through my veins. It's truly my life purpose! I want you to take a moment and ask yourself, "What is your life purpose? This is your one obligation in life. It's essential to find your purpose because it's what you have been put on this planet to do, it's the reason why you were born into this world.

Remember I mentioned at the start of this book that we are each born with a life purpose? Perhaps you have not found it yet and you are still wrestling to see it. You can ask God or your Higher Power or the Universe for clarity and guidance. In the Bible, Matthew 7:7-8 says, "Ask, and it will be given to you; seek, and you will find; knock, and it will be opened to you. For everyone who asks receives, and he who seeks finds, and to him who knocks, it will be opened."

You have the choice to create a life with purpose– a life where you have the energy that drives you to do incredible things and create a truly amazing existence. You will eventually find your life purpose. The person who you are and the events that have shaped your life in the past have always been leading you towards your true calling.

Another way to find your purpose is to create a 'Love List' of everything you love and makes you really happy. Is it fashion? Sports? Working with kids? Public speaking? Art? Health and wellness? Once you have your list, you can create a vision board with all the gifts and talents you have. A vision board is a fun, creative tool used to help you concentrate on a specific life goals. Creating vision boards helps identify your vision and gives clarity towards your life purpose. When you create a vision board, make sure to place it somewhere that you will see it often. You'll also find it helpful to practice your favorite affirmations in this book while looking at your vision board.

I've shared 111 affirmations in this book for you to use daily but creating a few of your own that are personal to you is a rewarding feeling as well. Once you've decided on the affirmations that you feel will work best for you, write them down and try your best to memorize them.

Many people experience greater amounts of success when standing in front of a mirror to read their affirmations aloud, but you can read them in the manner that makes you feel comfortable. When you are saying your daily affirmations, it's important that you are as relaxed as you can be. You only need to spend five minutes a day on your affirmations for them to be effective.

Having a positive attitude can work wonders when it comes to changing your outlook on life. By creating a list of affirmations, you can improve your positivity. The changes may not happen immediately, but the more you stand in front of the mirror and repeat your daily affirmations, the sooner you will notice a positive shift in your attitude. This shift will not only improve your own life, but it will improve the lives of those around you, as well. Affirmations attract positivity and wash away fear, doubt, and negative self-talk. Take time to pray, connect with God or your Higher Power and share your fears and ask for guidance. God gives wisdom to everyone who asks Him. In fact, He loves it when we come to Him with our concerns. God allows us to go through difficult challenges because those very experiences shape us for success. Even in the midst of pain, we can press on and not allow fear to take over.

We each have a chance for a fresh start. Every day is a new beginning. When you find the essence of how you want to feel and then infuse those feelings with what you want to have, you become a powerful creator of your own life's outcomes. When trying to create the life you want, try to think about the experiences that truly make you happy. The reality is that going through life and all of its ups and downs can destroy us if we allow it to, but through all of the trials and tribulations these experiences can sometimes allow us to discover our true purpose in life.

Remember, there is only one person responsible and fully accountable for making this year your best year ever and creating the life that you want. That person is YOU. Tomorrow is a gift, not a promise. Make today your fresh start.

Life Lesson #11:

The more you believe in yourself, the less you need others to. Today is all you have, so dream big. You have to find what you love doing. If you haven't yet, stop everything and figure it out.

What is your life purpose? If money wasn't an issue, write down what you would do with your life.

_____

_____

_____

_____

_____

_____

_____

_____

_____

_____

_____

_____

_____

_____

_____

Affirmations for New Beginnings

102. Today, I choose to move past my failures.

103. I am an intelligent being. I don't know everything, but today I choose to be open to new possibilities.

10.4 Today, nothing stands between me and my goals. I am fearless, courageous, and unstoppable.

105. Today, I choose to be open to all new opportunities that come my way.

106. Today, I choose to focus on my passions.

107. Today, I choose to chase opportunities.

108. This is the beginning of new experiences and knowl- edge.

109. I love myself unconditionally. I see the beauty in stopping to appreciate my blessings.

110. Today, I choose to start each day as a blank page and write my own destiny.

111. My behaviour creates my outcome. Today, I set the intention to love myself and in turn, love the world.

A Time for Reflection

Think about it... when is the perfect time for new beginnings? For you to finally start something new? Is fear stopping you from chasing your dreams or from creating the life you truly want? Don't let doubt, worry, and anxiety stop you from making this year your best year ever. Move beyond your fears. Don't allow fear to be your limitation. Make a conscious effort not to integrate fears of the unknown into your decision-making. There's never a best time to do something difficult, so trust that *the time is now* and it's never too late for a fresh start and to live out your life purpose to greatness.

A Time for Reflection is a place where you can make notes. You can use the bonus journal in the back of this book.

Take some time to write daily affirmations that resonate with you and set aside 5 minutes each day to say them out loud. You can select your favorite affirmations from this book, search for a few online that jump out at you or feel free to be creative and put together some of your own.

* Take a moment to reflect on the life lessons that you have experienced in your life. Perhaps there are a few of them in this book you can really relate to. Is there a particular life lesson that you need to revisit and work on this year? Maybe there's more than one and that's ok. Try to only focus on 1 or 2 at a time so that you don't become overwhelmed and give up all together. Start with 1 and work your way up to the next.

* Take a moment and reflect on your goals. Write down at least 3 goals that you want to work on over the next few days. Now take it a step further and write down the goals you want to reach this month. Leap even further again

and ask yourself where do you see yourself in 1 year from now? In 5 years from now? Write as many that come to mind.

* Think about the things and the people that make you really happy. Write down the things that you are grateful for. Make your "Love List".

* Self-care is an activity that we do deliberately in order to take care of our mental, emotional, and physical health. And it's something we very often overlook when we are trying to reach our goals. It's also essential to a good relationship with yourself and others and is fundamental for creating the life you want. It sets the tone for a great year ahead. Reflect on the word self-care. What words come to mind? What are some of the things that stop you from practicing self-care?

* Use the S.E.L.F. C.A.R.E. acronym below that I created to remind you of the importance of help self-care and self- love. I created this to help guide you and keep you on track.

"S" stands for Say no to the things or people that no longer serve you.

"E" stands for Exercise and making your health a priority.

"L" stands for Logging off from social media, unplugging from emails and texts and focusing on you.

"F" stands for Finances. Having your f inancials in order minimizes any unnecessary stress and worry.

"C" stands for Commitment. Be committed to making a change and reaching your goals.

"A" stands for Affirmations. Declare them daily in front of a mirror with intention.

"R" stands for Relax. Set aside some time to do the things you enjoy.

"E" stands for Eating well. Ensure you have a balanced diet and nutrition plan.

Reflect on my SELF-CARE acronym and makes notes about the areas outlined above that you want to improve on this year. Self-care reduces stress and assists as you move closer to your goals

* Do you know your life purpose? Take time to reflect on what makes you happy. What is your passion? You have the freedom to create the life you want.

Remember, we cannot open new doors with old keys. We need to walk down new paths to get to where we want to be. Every story in our life has an ending, but endings are opportunities to a fresh start. Don't hold on to what didn't grow last season. Plant your dreams in the soil of new beginnings. Find closure and move forward from a period of pain, failure, loss, or grief. Don't spend time grieving that you have not moved forward on making your goals come true. These memories are holding you back from experiencing a fully joyful life. Isn't your happiness worth starting over or starting fresh? It's time to move away from the darkness of your doubts. It's time to step in the light of possibility. What are you waiting for? Take that leap. Place your trust into the Universe, and new, beautiful things will manifest.

Let today be a Fresh Start. It's a new day, a new beginning. Let go of the past, forget what has gone, look forward to the opportunities. What does tomorrow hold? We will never know. The time is now to make this the best year ever and to create the life you want.

Revelations 21:5 "I am making everything new."

Acknowledgments

Aspecialthankyoutothosewhotooktheirtimeandcametogether to create the beautiful book cover and to the people who supported me during this journey and helped my vision of this book become a reality. I would thank you from the bottom of my heart, but for each of you, my heart has no bottom.

Aaron Mouland, Reiki Healer, Photography

Amber L.M. Beito, Consultant, Composition

Andrea Bourque, Madame Bling, Flawless Image, Celebrity Stylist

Brenda Konwisarz, Owner of Naked Bodyz Fashion, Wardrobe

Christina Atkinson, Founder of Paper Love by Christina, Backdrop

Nelly James, Motivational Speaker, Author

Patricia Giankas, Score-Up, Financial Wellness Specialist

Richard Barrett, Discovering Diversity Publishing, Graphic Designer

Sheena Blake, CEO of Discovering Diversity Publishing, Coaching

Taylor Made, Accountability Coach, Motivational Speaker, Author

T'kehya Prentice-Cupid, Founder of TK Natural Hair Wigs, Hairstylist

Wayne Mouland, Founder of Echo Movement, Visionary Philosopher

Bonus Journal

This complimentary journal is a gift from me to you! Yes, you heard right, totally free, on me. I am honoured that you took the time and purchased this book; therefore, I want to take this opportunity to thank you. *"Why a journal?"* you may ask and not a stack of cash? Ok, fair that's a question. I see how cash would be pretty awesome, but honestly, as nice as that would be, this journal is the next best thing! I promise! There's many benefits of journaling that I want to share with you and I encourage you to use this private creative space daily.

The advantages of journaling are that you are able to look back at the pages you've written and think about how far you have come. It helps create a clearer roadmap to your future. I want you to set aside time each day to write down your feelings, accomplishments and set backs. This practice acts as a release and can be very cleansing. Like a detox! Keeping a journal helps you establish order when your whole world feels like it's in chaos. If you are able to put your anxieties, frustrations and pains on paper, then you are less likely to bottle them up inside. As you write your goals daily, they will remain in your subconscious mind. Eventually, your fears and inhibitions will fade and your dreams and vision will quickly become your reality. Remember, you are the author of your life's story. You hold the pen. You have the power to create whatever life you want. As the designer of your world, this is your moment to express yourself, be vulnerable. As you write you immediately eliminate stress and improve your mental health. This journal is your safe place, it's a judgement free zone, write as if no one's watching

Some times what we need is a dose of encouragement and Karen Carrington, the "Energizer", delivers just that! She is an Inter- national Inspirational Speaker, Talk Show Host, Mental Health Advocate, Mother, Author and is a recipient of the 2017 Top 100 Black Women to Watch in Canada Award. Karen inspires others by sharing her personal journey of battling General Anxiety Disorder and re- building her life after divorce. She is a full time Executive Assistant, Certified Trainer, has successfully completed the Helix Entrepreneur Innovation Program at Seneca College and holds a Proficiency in French Diploma. Karen Carrington is known for delivering a high energy message which leaves people feeling rejuvenated, and restored. She captivates the audience with her authenticity as she shares her story of overcoming life tribulations with her candid humourous communication style. Her life purpose is speaking her truth to the masses in order to help people realize their own true potential.

e-mail: info@karencarrington.com
website: www.karencarrington.com

Made in the USA
Monee, IL
13 April 2022

94655519R00079